WALKING THE REZ ROAD

WALKING THE REZ ROAD

STORIES

JIM NORTHRUP

FULCRUM

GOLDEN, COLORADO

Library of Congress Cataloging-in-Publication Data
Northrup, Jim, 1943-
  Walking the Rez Road : stories / Jim Northrup.
    pages cm
  ISBN 978-1-55591-977-1
  1. Indians of North America--Minnesota--Literary collections. 2. Vietnam War, 1961-1975--Literary collections. 3. Ojibwa Indians--Literary collections. I. Title.
  PS3564.O765W3 2013
  818'.5409--dc23
                 2013003986

Printed in the United States of America
0 9 8 7 6 5 4 3 2 1

Design by Jack Lenzo

Fulcrum Publishing
4690 Table Mountain Dr., Ste. 100
Golden, CO 80403
800-992-2908 • 303-277-1623
www.fulcrumbooks.com

To Patricia,
Joseph Anthony Northrup (1886-1947),
Megan Noodin, Susan Stanich,
and all the elders and the little ones to come.

CONTENTS

INTRODUCTION

Twenty years ago, in the introduction to the first edition, I wrote, "*Walking the Rez Road* is a lesson in telling time." Many minutes and lessons later it is still true, and with a new edition it is worth asking, *aaniin endaso dibaaganeg noongwa* (what time is it now)?

Noongwa Chibinesi oshki-biidaabi-dibaajimowaan. Today Jim Northrup's writing marks a new dawn of Anishinaabe language and narration. He is known throughout the world as a journalist, storyteller, poet, and playwright. He is a father, grandfather, uncle, cousin, and *Anishinaabe Ogichidaa* whose voice is recognized for both its humor and humanity. His books are read in many college courses and are dog-eared and beloved fixtures in many homes along the rez road. He has shaped the field of Native American Literary Studies and inspired a generation of Anishinaabe scholars, earning his own honorary doctorate in 2012. In a continental context, Northrup's stories belong to the tradition of N. Scott Momaday, Leslie Marmon Silko, James Welch, Tom King, Thompson Highway, Joseph Boyden, and other modern Native American writers in Canada and the United States. The poetry that punctuates *Walking the Rez Road* echoes the style of Joy Harjo's lyrical descriptions of growing up Indian in America and Adrian Louis's harsh honesty about breaking fences, rules, and habits on a Dakota reservation. In an ancient context, Northrup's images are of the rock genre, clear marks of collective presence in the woods that thrive beside the Mississippi River and Great Lakes.

Noongwa ensa niibiing gekinomaawaan. Each summer now, Northrup hosts hundreds of students and teachers at the *Nahgachiwanong Ojibwemowin Maamawinigewin* (Fond du Lac Language Gathering). He believes in the connection between the culture and identity of the Anishinaabe people and works to ensure its revitalization. Even his first book, which was the first edition of *Walking the Rez Road*, hints at the importance of learning and using the language of the ancestors. Although the spellings have changed over time, the words he included in his earliest poems and stories still represent the core of his continually increasing knowledge of the language. *Wiigwaas, maanomin, wewiibtaan* . . . these words introduce readers to tree skins, precious food, and the short distance between tomorrow and today. Several of his poems have been translated into Ojibwemowin and appear here in the additional materials as an alternate version for students of the language.

Noongwa Chibinesi maamiikwendaan niibinaa gego. Northrup dares to remember. His poetry recalls the fights and racism of boarding school, but it also records the triumph of survival. He allows raw fear and haunting echoes to mingle with the pride and bravery of serving in Vietnam. As the poems and stories of *Walking the Rez Road* illustrate, he shares both his pain and tenderness, and in so doing invites readers to reconsider the world around them. Many have asked if Luke Warmwater is Jim Northrup, and in some ways he is, but in other ways he is only a character in series of complex stories artfully constructed by an author able to blend many personalities together while also holding some things close to his own heart. At the end of this volume, a bit of reality appears in the form of journalistic essays published between 1993 and 1995. These editorial opinions introduce the issues that defined the latter part of the twentieth century and set the agenda for the third millennium.

Noongwa n'gii niizhimi epiichi waayaabmose ishgoniga-nong. Two decades ago, Jim Northrup invited me to edit his first book and begin a journey. We are still walking the rez round, tracing the circles of life, and teaching others, and reminding ourselves, that stories involve listening as much as telling. In the 1990s we looked back to the 1970s for inspiration, rallying to keep the culture and practices alive. Now, in 2013, we look forward to the children and imagine them carrying the language and laughter forward in a new way . . . not just in the four directions, but in a way that ripples to the heavens and the very core of *Anishinaabe-aakiing*, connecting ancient stars with future heartbeats as we invite readers to walk the rez road.

Margaret Noodin, 2013

GLOSSARY OF OJIBWE WORDS

anin, *hello*
ayah, *yes*
bajeeshkaogan, *tipi*
bindigen, *come in*
boochigoo, *they had to do it anyway*
boujou neej, *hello, friend*
chimook, *white man*
gawain, *no*
mahnomin, *wild rice*
megwetch, *thank you*
ogichidag, *warriors*
Shinnob, slang, *from whence lowered the male of the species*
Um pa o wasta we, Dakota words for *beautiful daybreak woman*
waboose, *rabbit*
Wahbegan, Ojibwe name
weegwas, *birch bark*
wewiibitaan, *hurry up*

POEMS
AND STORIES

shrinking away

Survived the war, but was
having trouble surviving
the peace, couldn't sleep
more than two hours
was scared to be
without a gun.
Nightmares, daymares
guilt and remorse
wanted to stay drunk
all the time.
1966 and the VA said
Vietnam wasn't a war.
They couldn't help but
did give me a copy of
the yellow pages.
Picked a shrink off
the list. Fifty bucks an
hour, I was making 125
a week. Spent six
sessions establishing
rapport, heard about his
military life,
his homosexuality,

his fights with his mother,
and anything else he wanted
to talk about.
At this rate, we would have
got to me in 1999.
Gave up on that shrink
couldn't afford him and he
wasn't doing me any good.
Six weeks later, my shrink,
killed himself. Great.
Not only guilt about the
war but new guilt about
my dead shrink.
If only I had a better job,
I could have kept on
seeing him.
I thought we were making
real progress, maybe in another
six sessions, I could have
helped him.
I realized then that surviving
the peace was up to me.

OPEN HEART WITH A GRUNT

Luke Warmwater was doing his part as a grunt in South Vietnam. It was hot and humid. The monsoon was coming just over the mountains. It was getting close to the scary dark time that was also protective.

Luke and a couple other grunts happened to be near the Battalion Aid Station. Somebody, somewhere, must have stepped in some shit. The wounded and other marines were being carried in. They didn't recognize any of them, but it was hard to tell because they look so different when they're dead and wounded.

A TV news crew at the aid station was filming the stretchers and ponchos filled with wounded, dead, or dying marines. The grunts didn't like that. The news crew was easily persuaded not to do that when faced by three heavily armed field marines. The look in the marines' eyes indicated they had all used these tools of war recently.

The news crew disappeared as the grunts pitched in to help. The Viet Cong decided to liven things up with automatic weapons and mortars. Mortar rounds were walking closer to the Battalion Aid Station. The explosion sound was followed by a dirty cloud of dust and smoke. Green tracers began zipping through the perimeter. The grunts were a little worried when they saw these. They knew there were four rounds in between that you couldn't see. The tracers seemed to be mostly overhead, but the mortars continued their deadly fifty-meter steps through the area.

The marines returned fire with everything they had. This included rifles, machine guns, rocket launchers, 60 and 81mm mortars, and M-79 grenade launchers. The grunts knew that friendly artillery and helicopter gunships were just minutes away. Puff the Magic Dragon was also flying circles overhead.

Luke and the other grunts couldn't return fire because they were inside the perimeter. They were also busy carrying the marines who couldn't walk or would never walk again.

Luke was carrying a marine who had the gray color of death. He had been hit in the chest with a large projectile. The wound was about the size of a C ration can. He had other wounds that were bleeding.

Corpsmen and doctors began working on this guy right away. As they worked, the medical people crowded the grunts out of the way. The grunts were done carrying so they stood around and watched. The incoming fire seemed to be lightening up.

The marine's shirt was cut off and various things were hooked up to him. The grunts recognized plasma and a device that pumped air into the shattered chest. A doctor came running up. He seemed oblivious to the small arms fire and mortars. He used a scalpel to cut between the guy's ribs on the left side. He used his hands and a rib spreader to open the gray marine's chest. They couldn't hear the bones breaking because of the noise. The doctor reached in and began squeezing the guy's heart. There wasn't much blood visible as the procedure went on. The foot-wide trail of blood explained the lack of blood coming from the gray marine.

Medevac choppers began arriving, and their noise added to the confusion. Engine noise and the door gunners firing their M-60 machine guns drowned out the noise of incoming fire. The appearance of the choppers drew VC fire. A hovering chopper was too big of a target. The choppers were like deadly magnets as the VC mortars and machine gun rounds began hitting near them.

The grunts began loading up the choppers, taking only the wounded. The dead could wait until things settled down. The machine gun bullets hit the choppers with a characteristic sound that was easy to hear above the noise of the firefight. The gray marine was being carried on a stretcher as the doctor walked alongside, still squeezing. One grunt was handed the bag that pumped air; another was given the plasma and blood bags. Luke was given something to squeeze. It was the size of a tennis ball and it was connected to the guy somewhere. A corpsman told Luke and the other grunts their duties as the gray marine and his soggy stretcher were loaded on the chopper. The door gunner helped load the wounded between bursts from his machine gun.

Darkness added to the confusion as the overloaded chopper tried to lift off with its macabre cargo. The green tracers searched for the chopper as the pilot used forward momentum to gain altitude. The chopper floor was slippery with blood, and the noise was loud. It was semidark as they cleared the trees outside the perimeter.

The grunts looked out and down while assisting the doctor. The perimeter was lit up with flares, fires, and explosions. Luke saw a chopper struggling to get off the ground. Marines jumped out of the chopper and began carrying the wounded out.

Luke wanted to fire his rifle at an enemy machine gun plainly shooting at them. The tracers were almost pretty as they arced towards them. Luke couldn't shoot and squeeze at the same time, so he just tried to make himself as small as possible inside his flak jacket and helmet.

The door gunner began screaming as a round came through the floor. Blood squirted out of his leg as he screamed and fired his machine gun. Luke was able to get a battle dressing on the gunner's leg between squeezes.

Something happened to time. It no longer flowed. Time slowed down and the grunts were no longer aware, but their eyes, ears, and minds kept absorbing things as the chopper climbed out of rifle range.

Luke looked down at the gray marine. He didn't know him, but Luke realized it very easily could have been himself lying on that blood-soaked stretcher. Luke prayed for him. The doctor shouted encouraging words as they flew the twenty-five miles to Da Nang. The doctor said the guy was still alive, but the grunts doubted it, because once someone turned that color gray, they never came back.

The chopper landed and the wounded were carried into the operating rooms. Luke and the other grunts just stood around outside, trapped inside their minds with the memories of what they saw, heard, and felt. Time returned to normal as the doctor came out and told them the gray marine died on the table.

They got back into another chopper for the return to the scene of the firefight. This time they fired back as the chopper came in.

Luke still sees that gray marine in his nightmares every couple of months.

wahbegan

Didja ever hear a sound
smell something
taste something
that brought you back
to Vietnam, instantly?
Didja ever wonder
when it would end?
It ended for my brother.
He died in the war
but didn't fall down
for fifteen tortured years.
His flashbacks are over,
another casualty whose name
will never be on the Wall.
Some can find peace
only in death.
The sound of his
family crying hurt.
The smell of the flowers
didn't comfort us.
The bitter taste
in my mouth
still sours me.
How about a memorial
for those who made it
through the war
but still died
before their time?

MINE OF MINE

Hot, triple-digit heat and humidity. Wide-open rice paddies. South of Da Nang, east of An Hoa. It was a long, hot walk in the sun. For the grunts doing the walking, there was a heat casualty every thousand meters. The sound of the choppers coming and going was everywhere. When the noise faded for the last time, it got quiet and scary.

This was a pedestrian's nightmare. The worst place in the world to be a hiker. It was 1966 and Luke Warmwater was walking point. He was making his living by killing and trying to stay alive. To stay alive, he had to look for mines, punji pits, dud artillery shells, and enemy soldiers. One of the enemy soldiers was a sniper.

The sniper was good. Head shots only. The scuttlebutt said he would shoot only the third guy in line, always the third guy, and always in the head. Luke was walking point. He searched the trail and dangerous open spaces. He listened. He came to an open area. He got down and looked it over. The patrol behind him did likewise. They pointed their rifles toward opposite sides of the trail. Luke studied the terrain carefully. No sign of humans or danger.

He got up and stepped carefully into the sunlight, into the open. He was ready. His M-14 rifle was ready. The Vietnam War for him was very small, very personal. Luke's morals were on hold, so were his feelings. He thought of his trigger finger as the judge, jury, and executioner. Luke was a young killing machine trying to stay alive.

His right foot slipped down and outward. He froze and looked. He was staring down at his own funeral. Under his foot was a thin piece of wire wrapped around a twig.

The twig was bent. If he moved, it might explode. If he didn't move, it might explode. He looked closer. It was a mine, a foot trap. A shoebox-size hole dug into the ground. The hole was covered by a woven mat. It looked like the wire was connected to a grenade.

Now what? he thought. Out in the open, pinned by a mine. He started to think of ways to get off the mine. *Let's see now, I could put my helmet and flak jacket over the mine and dive away from the blast.* That wouldn't work, he might be diving on another mine. *I could just stay here and live out the rest of my life anchored to this mine,* he thought. That wouldn't work. The sniper might forget his third person rule. *I could shit in my pants,* he thought.

Luke thought of his family back home. What would they say if they knew he was about to lose a leg? For the ninety-ninth time that day he regretted volunteering for Vietnam. He wished he was back in Da Nang. He wished he was ten feet back in the shade. He wished he was anywhere but here, standing on this wire.

Sweat poured out and made his hands slippery. His wet fingers clutched the impotent rifle. The rifle that was useless against this kind of enemy.

Luke thought some more. *Does the guy behind me know what's going on here?* He couldn't talk, his throat was too dry. He hand-signaled the marine behind him. Luke pointed at his foot and made an exploding motion with his fingers. He froze again. Now would be a bad time for the dysentery to hit. Luke wondered if he could take a drink from his canteen without the device exploding. The water would taste good, even if it was just warm rice paddy water.

When he thought about water, he imagined a tall glass of ice water. He would have traded his prized air mattress for a chance to be anywhere else, drinking a tall glass of ice water. Anywhere but here, pinned by a mine. A mine that would drastically affect any plans for the future. His future that was measured in seconds, maybe minutes.

His leg muscles began to twitch. He wondered if this new movement would set off the mine. No sense dying dry, he thought. He drank half of his canteen. The mine didn't explode.

The marine walking behind came up. He was probing

the ground with his bayonet. He was looking for other mines. He didn't find any. He got to Luke and carefully moved the woven mat. No explosion. The twig was still bent. The wire was quivering. The quivering wire led to a grenade that was barely visible. The marine grabbed the wire. The device didn't explode. He looked up at Luke and said, "You can move your foot now."

"Really?" Luke croaked with a scratchy voice, barely audible.

"Really. I want to dig this one out. It'll make a good souvenir."

"Really?" Luke still couldn't believe it.

"Really. Let's get out of this open area."

"Really," said Luke as he pulled his now asleep leg from the wire.

The marine unscrewed the blasting cap and scraped the explosive from the grenade. Luke limped out of the open area. He looked for shade and checked the ground carefully before he sat down. He drained the rest of the water from his canteen and rubbed feeling back into his leg. The water tasted better than any he could imagine. His leg was tingling but was still there.

The marine was walking back to join Luke when the explosion happened. He disappeared in a cloud of dirty smoke. His crumpled body was thrown to the ground. Luke felt the rocks, dirt, and shrapnel hit his flak jacket and legs.

Luke saw the marine lying there. The missing lower leg and the amount of blood told Luke this marine was dying. They both had overlooked another mine.

Rifle fire came from the front and one flank. The explosion must have been the signal for the gooks to start shooting. Luke and the other grunts returned fire. The radioman called in artillery. The enemy fire slowed and stopped except for an occasional round. The marines quit shooting and began to redistribute their ammo.

Luke looked at the wounded guy. He crawled out to him. He was still moaning and bleeding. A rifle shot cracked as

Luke dragged him back under cover. By this time, the marine had stopped moaning because he was dead. The souvenir was still gripped in his lifeless fingers. Luke removed the grenade. He put it in his pack; this mine of mine, he thought. Luke held the dead marine's hand until a corpsman covered the body with a poncho.

A chopper came in to remove the dead marine. The chopper also brought ammo, food, and water. The war must go on, thought Luke.

The sound of a chopper caused Luke to turn his head. When he did, he realized he was not in Vietnam. It was 1986, and Luke was in Washington, DC. He was at the Wall, the Vietnam Veterans Memorial. He looked at the black reflective granite, name after name. Reading the names, he remembered hearing names read off when he was in the service: mail call, roll call, work details.

He had the flashback about the mine as he read the ten-foot panel of names. He had read the book of the dead so he knew he was at the right panel.

When he found the marine's name, he reached up and touched the letters cut into stone. When he did, he felt relieved, almost like he had been carrying a pack for the past twenty years and could now take it off. He offered tobacco as his eyes began to burn and fill with tears.

A bearded vet came over. He wore a faded camouflage jacket. His baseball cap proudly proclaimed that he was a Vietnam vet. He hugged Luke and said, "Welcome home, brother."

walking point

With his asshole puckered up tight
the marine was walking point.
He was hunting men
who were hunting him.

His rifle was in perfect order,
he wasn't—fear, fear of not
feeling fear, the heat, mud,
and mosquitoes all addled
his brain housing group
as he walked and thought along.

Thou shall not kill.
That stuff didn't work here.
God must have stayed
back in the real world.

Is any of this real?
Is this a green nightmare
I'm going to wake up from?

He sang to himself as
his senses gathered evidence
of his continued existence.

His eyes saw, his ears heard
his heart felt a numb nothing.
His mind analyzed it all as
he studied the trail.

He amused himself as he walked along.
The old story about bullets, ha,
don't sweat the ones that got your
name, worry about the ones addressed:
to whom it may concern.

On another level his mind churned with
rifle, M-14, gas-operated, magazine-fed
air-cooled, semi-automatic shoulder weapon
weight: 12 pounds with 20 rounds
sustained rate of fire: 30 rounds per minute
effective range: zero to 460 meters
or, hand grenade, M-26,
and so on and on and on. . .

Movement, something is moving up there.
Drop to the mud, rifle pointing at the unknown.
Looks like two of them, hunting him.
They have rifles, but he saw them first.
The marine corps takes over—
breathe, relax, aim, slack, squeeze.

The shooting is over in five seconds
the shakes are over in a halfhour
the memories are over never.

VETERAN'S DANCE

Don't sweat the small shit, Lug thought. It's all small shit unless they're shooting at you.

The tall, skinny Shinnob finished changing the tire on his car. It took longer than usual because he had to improvise with the jack. Summer in Minnesota and Lug, Luke Warmwater's cousin, was on his way to a powwow.

The powwow was on its second day. The dancers were getting ready for their third grand entry. Singers around the various drums had found their rhythm. Old bones were loosening up. The MC was entertaining the crowd with jokes. Some of the jokes brought laughs and others brought groans. Kids wove through the people that circled the dance arena. The drum sound knitted the people together.

Lug brushed his long hair away from his face as he looked into the sky for eagles. He had been away from home a long time and was looking forward to seeing his friends and relatives again.

Although he didn't dance, he really enjoyed powwows. Lug was content to be with his people again. Ever since the war, he felt disconnected from the things that made people happy.

The first time he walked around the arena he just concentrated on faces. He was looking for family. While walking along, he grazed at the food stands. He smelled, then sampled the fry bread, moose meat, and wild rice soup.

The Shinnobs walking around the dance arena looked like a river flowing two directions. Groups of people would stop and talk. Lug smiled at the laughing circles of Shinnobs. He looked at faces and eyes.

That little one there, she looked like his sister Judy when she was that age. Lug wondered if he would see her here. Judy was a jingledress dancer and should be at this powwow. After all, she lived only a mile away from the powwow grounds.

The guy walking in front of him looked like his cousin who had gone to Vietnam. Nope, couldn't be him. Lug had heard that he died in a single-car accident last fall.

Sitting in a red-and-white-striped powwow chair was an old lady who looked like his grandma. She wore heavy brown stockings held up with a big round knot at the knees. She chewed Copenhagen and spit the juice in a coffee can just like his gram. Of course, Lug's grandma had been dead for ten years, but it was still a good feeling to see someone who looked like her.

Lug recognized the woman walking toward him. She was his old used-to-be girlfriend. He hoped she didn't want to talk about what went wrong with them. She didn't, just snapped her eyes and looked away. Lug knew it was his fault he couldn't feel close to anyone. His face was a wooden mask as they passed each other. He could feel her looking at him out of the corner of her eyes. Maybe, he thought, just maybe.

He stopped at a food stand called Stand Here. Lug had black coffee and a bag of minidonuts. The sugar and cinnamon coating stuck to his fingers. He brushed off his hands and lit a smoke. Lug watched the snaggers eight to sixty-eight cruising through the river of Shinnobs.

That jingledress dancer walking toward him looked like his sister Judy. Yup, it was her. The maroon dress made a tinkling, jingling sound as she came closer. She looks healthy, Lug thought. A few more gray hairs, but she moves like she was twenty years younger. They both smiled hard as their eyes met. Warm brown eyes reached for wary ones.

She noticed that the lines on his face were deeper. The lines fanned out from the edges of his eyes. He looked like he had lost some weight since the last time she had seen him. His blue jean jacket is just hanging on him, she thought.

Lug and Judy shook hands and hugged each other. Her black beaded bag hit him on the back as they embraced. They were together again after a long time apart. Both leaned back to get a better look at each other.

"C'mon over to the house when they break for supper," she said.

"Got any cornbread?" he asked.

"I can whip some up for you," she promised.

"Sounds good," he said.

Eating cornbread was a reminder of when they were young together. Sometimes it was the only thing to eat in the house. Cornbread was the first thing she made him when he came back from Vietnam.

"I have to get in line for the grand entry. So, I'll see you later. I want to talk to you about something," she said.

"Okay, dance a round for me," Lug said.

"I will, just like I always do."

Lug watched the grand entry. He saw several relatives in their dance outfits. He nodded to friends standing around the dance arena. Lug sipped hot coffee as the grand entry song was sung. Judy came dancing by. Lug turned and looked at his car.

He walked to it as the flag song started. He moved in time to the beat as he walked. Lug decided to get his tire fixed at the truck stop. He got in and closed the car door as the veteran's song came over the public address system.

Lug left the powwow grounds and slipped a tape in his cassette player. The Animals singing "Sky Pilot" filled the car. Lug sang along with the vintage music.

He drove to the truck stop and read the newspaper while the mechanic fixed his tire. Lug put the tire in his trunk, paid the guy, and drove to his sister's house. He listened to the Righteous Brothers do "Soul and Inspiration" on the way.

Judy's car was in the driveway so he knew she was home. He parked and walked up to the front door. Lug rang the doorbell and walked in. He smelled cornbread.

She was in the kitchen making coffee. He sat at the kitchen table as she took the cornbread out of the oven. The steaming yellow bread made his mouth moist. Judy poured him a cup of coffee and sat down at the table.

"How have you been?" she asked.

"Okay. My health is okay."

"Where have you been? I haven't heard from you in quite a while."

"Oh you know, just traveling here and there. I'd work a little bit and then move on. For awhile there I was looking for guys I knew in the war."

"Where was that you called from last March?" she asked.

"DC. I was in Washington, DC. I went to the Wall, and after being there, I felt like I had to talk to someone I knew."

"You did sound troubled about something."

"I found a friend's name on the Wall. He died after I left Vietnam. I felt like killing myself."

"I'm glad you didn't."

"Me too. We wouldn't be having this conversation if I had gone through with it."

She got up, cut the cornbread, and brought it to the table. He buttered a piece and began taking bites from the hot bread. She refilled his cup.

"Remember when we used to haul water when we were kids? I was thinking about it the other day, that one time it was thirty below and the cream cans fell off the sled? You somehow convinced me it was my fault. I had to pump the water to fill the cans again. You told me it was so I could stay warm. I guess in your own way you were looking out for me," she said.

"Nah, I just wanted to see if I could get you to do all the work." Lug smiled at his sister.

"I thought it was good of you to send the folks money from your first military paycheck so we could get our own pump. We didn't have to bum water from the neighbors after that."

"I had to. I didn't want you to break your back, lugging those cream cans around."

"Yah, I really hated wash days. Ma had me hauling water all day when she washed clothes."

She got up and got a glass of water from the kitchen faucet. As she came back to the table she said, "I've been talking to a spiritual leader about you. He wants you to come and see him. Don't forget to take him tobacco."

"That sounds like a good idea. I've been wanting to talk to someone," he said.

"What was it like in the war? You never talk much about it."

Lug stared deep into his black medicine water as if expecting an answer to scroll across. He trusted his sister, but it was still difficult talking about the terrible memories.

His eyes retreated into his head as he told her what happened to him, what he did in the war. She later learned that this was called the thousand-yard stare. His eyes looked like he was trying to see something far away. The laugh lines were erased from his face.

"Sometimes I'd get so scared I couldn't get scared anymore," he said, hunched over his coffee cup.

Judy touched his arm. Her face said she was ready to listen to her brother.

"One night they were shooting at us. No one was getting hurt. It got to be a drag ducking every time they fired. The gunfire wasn't very heavy, just a rifle round every couple of minutes. We didn't know if it was the prelude to a big attack or just one guy out there with a case of ammo and a hard-on. We laid in our holes, counted the rounds going by, and tried to shrink inside our helmets. The bullets went by for at least a half hour. I counted seventeen of them. The ones that went high made a buzzing noise. The close ones made a *crack* sound. First you'd hear the bullet go by, then the sound of where it came from.

"I got tired of that shit. I crawled out of my hole and just stood there. I wanted to see where the bad guy was shooting from. The guys in the next hole told me to get down, but I was in a fuck it mood. I didn't care what happened, didn't care if I lived or died."

Lug stood up to show his sister what it was like standing in the dark. He leaned forward trying to see through the night. His hands clutched an imaginary rifle. Lug's head swiveled back and forth as he looked for the hidden rifleman.

He jerked as a rifle bullet came close to him. He turned his head toward the sound.

Judy watched Lug. She could feel her eyes burning and the tears building up. Using only willpower, she held the tears back. Judy somehow knew the tears would stop the flood of memories coming out of her brother. She waited.

"I finally saw the muzzle flash. I knew where the bastard was firing from. After he fired the next time, we all returned fire. We must have shot five hundred rounds at him. The bad guy didn't shoot anymore. We either killed him or scared the shit out of him. After the noise died down, I started getting scared. I realized I could have been killed standing up like that."

He paused before speaking again.

"That shows you how dangerous a fuck it attitude is. I guess I have been living my life with a fuck it attitude."

Lug sat back down and reached for another piece of cornbread. He ate it silently. When he finished the cornbread, he lit a cigarette.

She touched his shoulder as she poured more coffee. Lug accepted this as permission to continue fighting the war. Judy sat down and lit her own cigarette.

"It was really crazy at times. One time we were caught out in this big rice paddy. They started shooting at us. I was close to the front of the formation so I got inside the tree line quick. The bad guys couldn't see me. When I leaned over to catch my breath, I heard the *snick, snick, bang* sound of someone firing a bolt-action rifle. The enemy soldier was firing at the guys still out in the rice paddy. I figured out where the bad guy was from the sound—*snick, snick, bang*. I fired a three-round burst at the noise. That asshole turned and fired at me. I remember the muzzle flash and the bullet going by together. I fired again as I moved closer. Through a little opening in the brush, I could see what looked like a pile of rags, bloody rags. I fired another round into his head. We used to do that all the time—one in the head to make sure. The 7.62 bullet knocked his hat off. When the hat came off, hair came spilling out. It was a woman."

Lug slumped at the kitchen table, unable to continue his story. He held his coffee cup as if warming his hands. Judy sat there looking at him. Tears ran down her cheeks and puddled up on the table.

Lug coughed and lit a cigarette. Judy reached for one of her own, and Lug lit it for her. Their eyes met. She got up to blow her nose and wipe her eyes. Judy was trembling as she came back and sat at the table. She wanted to cradle her brother but couldn't.

"Her hair looked like grandma's hair used to look. Remember her long, black, shiny hair? This woman had hair like that. I knew killing people was wrong somehow, but this made it worse when it turned out to be a woman."

Lug slowly rocked his head back and forth.

When it looked like Lug was not going to talk anymore, Judy got up and opened the back door. She poured more coffee and sat there looking at him. He couldn't meet her eyes.

"Tell me how you got wounded; you never did talk about it. All we knew was that you won a Purple Heart," she probed.

After a long silence, Lug answered, "Ha, won a Purple Heart? We used to call them Idiot Awards. It meant that you fucked up somehow. Standing in the wrong place at the wrong time, something like that."

Lug's shoulders tightened as he began telling her about his wounds. He reached down for his leg.

"I don't know what happened to my leg. It was a long firefight, lots of explosions. After it was over, after the medevac choppers left, we were sitting around talking about what happened.

"I looked down and noticed blood on my leg. I thought it was from the guys we carried in from the listening post. The pain started about then. I rolled up my pants and saw a piece of shrapnel sticking out. Doc came over and pulled it out. He bandaged it up and must have written me up for a Heart. I remember it took a long time to heal because we were always in the water of the rice paddies."

Lug was absently rubbing his leg as he told his sister about his wound.

He suddenly stood up and changed the subject. He didn't talk about his other wounds. He drained his cup.

"I gotta go. I think I talked too much already. I don't want you to think I am crazy because of what I did in the war. I'll see you at the powwow," said Lug, walking to the door.

As she looked at his back, she wished there was something she could do to ease his memories of the war.

"Wait a minute," Judy told her brother.

She lit some sage and smudged him with an eagle feather. He stood there with his eyes closed, palms facing out.

He thanked her and walked out the door.

While cleaning up after her brother left, Judy remembered the ads on TV for the Vet's Center. She looked the number up in the book and called. Judy spoke to a counselor who listened. The counselor suggested an inpatient post-traumatic stress disorder program.

The closest one was located in St. Cloud, Minnesota. Judy got the address for her brother.

She went back to the powwow and found Lug standing on the edge of the crowd.

"They have a program for treating PTSD," she told Lug.

"Yah, I saw something on TV about PTSD."

"What did you think of it? What do you think of entering a treatment program?"

"It might do some good. I was talking to a guy who went through it. He said it helped him. It might be worth a shot," Lug said.

"I talked to a counselor after you left. She said you can come in anytime."

"How about right now? Do you think they are open right now?"

"Sure, they must keep regular hours."

When she saw him walking to his car, she thought. *It didn't take much to get him started.*

Lug left the powwow and drove to the Vet's Center. On the way he listened to Dylan singing "Blowin' in the Wind."

At the Vet's Center, Lug found out he could enter the program in a couple of days. His stay would be about a month.

Lug talked to the spiritual man before he went in for the program. He remembered to bring him a package of Prince Albert tobacco and a pair of warm socks.

In talking with the man, Lug learned that veterans were respected because of the sacrifices they had made in the war. The man told Lug he would pray for him. He told Lug to come back and see him when he got out of the Veteran's Hospital.

Lug went to see the counselor, and she helped him complete the paperwork. He thanked her and drove to his sister's house. He parked his car and went inside. Judy showed him where he could leave his car parked while he was gone.

Judy drove Lug to the brick hospital. Lug took his bag of clothes and walked up the steps. Judy waved from her car. Lug noticed she was parked under an American flag.

He walked into the building. The smell of disinfectant reminded him of other official buildings he had been through.

Lug was ready for whatever was to come. Don't sweat the small shit, he thought.

Lug quickly learned that he was not the only one having trouble coping with memories of the war. He felt comfortable talking with other vets who had similar experiences.

Living in the Vet's Hospital felt like being in the military again. He slept in a warm bed and ate warm food. Lug spent most of his time with guys his age who had been to Vietnam. His time was structured for him.

In the group therapy sessions they told war stories at first. After a while together they began to talk about feelings. Lug became aware that he had been acting normally in what was an abnormal situation. He felt like he was leaving some of his memories at the hospital.

In spite of the camaraderie he felt, Lug was anxious to

rejoin his community. He wanted to go home. Lug knew he would complete the program but didn't expect to spend one extra minute at the hospital.

While he was gone, Judy was busy. She made Lug a pair of moccasins. The toes had the traditional beaded floral design. Around the cuffs she stitched the colors of the Vietnam campaign ribbon. She called the counselor at the Vet's Center to make sure the colors were right. It was green, then yellow with three red stripes, yellow, then green again. The smoke-tanned hide smell came to her as she sewed.

The hardest part was going down in the basement for the trunk her husband left when he went to Vietnam. The trunk contained his traditional dance outfit. It had been packed away since he hadn't come back from the war.

Judy drove to the hospital and picked up Lug when he completed the PTSD program. Looks like he put on some weight, she thought when she first saw him.

She drove to the spiritual man's house. They were listening to a powwow tape while driving. Lug tapped his hand on his knee in time to the drum. On the way, Lug told hospital stories. She could see his laugh lines as he talked about the month with other vets.

At the house, Judy waited outside while the two men talked and smoked. She listened to both sides of the tape twice before Lug came out. He had a smile and walked light on his feet. Lug got in the car.

Judy drove to her house. They listened to the powwow on the way. She could see that he was enjoying the music.

"I've got that extra bedroom downstairs. You can stay there until you get your own place," she told him.

"Sounds like a winner. Cornbread every day?"

"Nope, special occasions only."

"I might be eligible for a disability pension, but I'd rather get a job," Lug said.

"Do what you want to do," she said.

"Where are we going now?" Lug asked.

"We're going to a powwow. I got my tent set up already, and I want to dance in the first grand entry."

"Okay. It'll feel good to see familiar faces again."

"Did the hospital do anything for you?" she asked.

"I think so, but it felt better talking to the spiritual man," he answered.

When they got to the powwow grounds, Judy drove to her tent. Lug perched on the fender when she went inside to change into her jingledress.

Sure, the hospital was nice, but it feels better being here with relatives, Lug thought. He breathed the cool air in deeply. He could hear his sister's jingledress as she got dressed. He was trying to decide which food stand to start with when his sister came out.

"Tie this up for me, will you?" she asked.

Judy handed him the eagle fluff and medicine wheel. He used rawhide to tie it to her small braid. After she checked to make sure it was the way she wanted it, Judy said, "Go in the tent and get your present."

"Okay," he said, jumping off the fender and unzipping the tent.

Inside the tent he saw a pair of moccasins on top of a traditional dance outfit. The colors of the campaign ribbon on the moccasins caught his eye. He took off his sneakers and put on the moccasins.

"Hey, thanks a lot. I needed some moccasins," said Lug.

"The rest of the outfit belongs to you too," she said.

"Really?" He recognized the dance outfit. He knew who used to own it. He thought of his brother-in-law and the Vietnam War.

"Hurry up and put it on. It's almost time for grand entry," Judy told him.

Lug put on the dance outfit and walked out for the inspection he knew she would give. He did a couple of steps to show her how it fit. She smiled her approval.

They walked to where the people were lining up. He was

laughing as he joined the traditional dancers. He saw his cousin Fuzzy, who was a Vietnam vet.

"Didja hear? They got a new flavor for Vietnam vets," Lug said.

"Yah, what is it?" asked Fuzzy, who had been in Khe Sahn in '68.

"Agent Grape," said Lug.

They both laughed at themselves for laughing.

Lug danced the grand entry song with slow dignity. He felt proud. Lug moved with the drum during the flag song.

When the veteran's song began, Lug moved back to join his sister. Both of them had tears as they danced the veteran's honor song together.

rez car

It's seventeen years old.
It's been used
a lot more than most.
It's louder than a 747.
It's multicolored and none
of the tires are brothers.
I'm the 7th or 8th owner
I know I'll be the last.
What's wrong with it?
Well, the other day
the steering wheel fell off.
The radio doesn't work
but the heater does.
The seats have seen more
asses than a proctologist.
I turn the key, it starts.
I push the brake, it stops.
What else is a car
supposed to do?

WORK ETHIC

Now that ricing was over, Luke Warmwater began to think about getting through winter. What he needed was a job. A job to pay for food, child support, and recreational drugs. He also thought he would need a winter jacket, boots, and mitts. His old car had snow tires from last year. It had three of them still on.

After thinking about working in the woods, cutting firewood, Luke remembered wading through the ass-deep snow, digging out frozen birch with frozen fingers. No, it seemed like an inside job was the answer to the problem at hand.

Luke went to the state employment office because he heard they sometimes had a line on available jobs. After looking at the list of jobs open to any Sawyer Indian who was a chemical engineer or a technical sales representative, he narrowed his choices to the ones he thought he could bullshit his way into.

The one that called for a management trainee looked promising. It was a hamburger franchise, and if nothing else, he would be near food during the cold days coming. With his referral slip in hand, he made it to the interview with three minutes to spare. He interpreted this as a good sign.

The manager got things off to a bad start when he asked if Luke would cut his hair for the job. The only other choice was to wear a hairnet like his grandma wore. He didn't want to smell like hamburgers, and a daily diet of fast food would get pretty tiring after a while, so the career of retail food sales was out.

The next referral slip directed him to report to the personnel office of a large pizza-making factory. He filled out the forms, and the secretary told him to report for the second shift. He didn't know he automatically qualified for the job when he was able to fill out the forms without assistance.

His first night on the job went okay. He was given a pushbroom and told which areas to sweep. He thought, not too bad; the broom wasn't heavy and the building was warm. He also thought, I never really noticed the smell of pizza before.

After steering the broom around for a couple of hours, he began to think of ways to advance from this menial, manual labor. The next time the foreman came by, Luke asked about it. The foreman showed him a guy who was sweeping around the next conveyor belt. The foreman said the guy had been there for almost a year and at the next opening would be promoted to the production line.

Luke took a closer look at his fellow workers and came to the conclusion that some of them were from a sheltered workshop someplace.

At the lunch break of pizza, he tried to strike up a conversation with some of the other workers. The conversation didn't get very far unless he spoke in one-syllable words, nodded his head, and smiled a lot. He got tired of the vacant smiles, and when he noticed he was beginning to smile like that, he thought of other jobs he could handle.

He knew that the Indian Center always had a job or two in one of their programs. With resume in hand, he showed up to meet the screening committee. The screening committee was all white and most of them looked like ex-radicals or ex-hippies. These former flower children had gone "to help the Indians" and were now in positions of authority at the Indian Center. The positions they held were probably the first rung on the ladder of success.

In spite of the brilliant answers he gave during the interview, he didn't have a prayer of getting the job. He didn't know it then, but one member of the screening committee had a friend that needed a job. While waiting for the phone call about the job, he remembered the story of the Indian who showed up for an interview wearing a blond wig. Neither one of them got the job.

Luke was getting desperate and thought he'd either have to get a job or pull a job. He knew if he didn't make a child support payment pretty soon, the court would repossess him and put him in jail for a least ninety days. This wouldn't get him all the way through winter, so he continued his job-seeking efforts.

While walking through the shopping mall, he noticed a new water bed store opening up. He went in and asked for a job. The sales manager had a great idea for a marketing gimmick. Luke got the job. His job was to sleep on a water bed in the front window of the store. This was all too good to be true, and Luke had trouble falling asleep the first couple of days on the job. He wondered if he was sleeping open-mouthed, if he was drooling or thrashing around while he slept. He got used to people staring at him because this new job was a dream. He could party all night and still get up and go to work. Luke's job ended when he was caught demonstrating another use of the water bed to the sales manager's wife.

By this time the long arm of the law reached out and snagged Luke. It was about his child support, and unless Luke came up with the money, the judge would see that he had a warm place to sleep in the county jail. The judge sitting on the bench knew Luke from their previous encounters. He didn't want to send him off to be fed and sheltered at county expense. The judge proposed a solution. Luke began to work around the judge's house as a handyman. He figured the judge wouldn't get mad if he charged up a rifle and shells where the judge did business. He was wrong, and after getting an ear beating about trust and credit, he found himself back on the street, looking for a job. He did get to keep the rifle and shells, though.

He finally found a job at a machine shop. This one paid better than all the others. With the income, he paid the judge for the rifle and shells. He caught up on his child support. He ate good. He began to look at the finer things in life. One of the finer things in life was a different car.

His old car was loud, drank oil, and the missing window made the wind chill unbearable. He hated to take it to the scrap yard, but took small pleasure in knowing he was the last person to ever drive the car.

The job at the machine shop was pretty easy. He drilled four holes in a piece of metal. After a little time on the job, he was able to get his entire day's quota done right after lunch. The money was good, and it was warm in the building, so he hung in there for the rest of the winter.

One fine spring day after lunch Luke was looking out the window. He thought how good it would feel to have the sun shining on his face. He reached over and shut off the machine. He thought back to how close he and the machine had become. He was the part of the machine that went home at night. He went out the door, never to return.

Luke had a cousin who was a pusher on a big construction project. He thought his cousin could get him on at that job.

Yep, next week he'd look up his cousin.

death two

We went for a ride up the
oldest Minnesota state lottery
two-lane Highway Two
grain trucks, logging trucks.
Drove by the ash swamps
some trees tipped over
showing us the death part
of their life cycle
grain trucks, logging trucks.
Black ravens, shiny wings
catching the weak December sun
flew with us a while
grain trucks, logging trucks.
Orange snowplows, waiting
 to continue the winter war
with salt, sand, steel plows
grain trucks, logging trucks.
Paper mills, power plants
making visible steam and
invisible pollution
grain trucks, logging trucks.

Caught a chill when a
semi suddenly filled the
rear view mirror,
he passed us on a curve
wasn't our turn to die
grain trucks, logging trucks.
We drove over the frozen
coils of the Mississippi
wondered how it felt
to live downstream
grain trucks, logging trucks.
Took our chances on the
oldest lottery back home again
we avoided headlights, taillights,
grain trucks, logging trucks,
and just followed the stars home.

BLOODY MONEY

Luke Warmwater was broke. Not short of money, but broke. The kind of broke that is all pervading. Everyone he knew was waiting for a check; not him though.

He knew there was nothing coming down the road for him. The ship he was waiting for must have sunk. He was so broke he had to mix his metaphors so he'd have enough. He was so broke he was telling stories about a guy he knew who had a dollar.

But, as the man said, he was broke, not poor.

He had a solution in mind. Moneyless Luke went down to the bleeders at the blood donor center. He had heard this place was called Dr. Dracula's Bank. He also heard the workers there were called vampires.

He thought about the whole thing before he went through the door. If blood plasma was worth ten dollars, what was the value of his other bodily fluids? What was the going rate for earwax? Does anyone buy spit or sweat? What about live bile? Where do you donate sperm?

The cheerful mood of the vampires worried him. How can a person be so happy to make others bleed? The bright lights of the place showed him some of the plasma producers.

They all looked like people who needed ten dollars. That was the common thread running through them. There were hippies, winos, Indians, street people, college students, blacks, and some who defied a label.

The vampires looked like they were all stamped from the same mold. The white uniforms and artificial smiles made them look alike. The vampires acted like the people selling plasma were some kind of livestock. They were efficient as they went about their duties. Luke had seen the same look on farmers' faces as they milked their cows.

Luke entered the process. First was a blood test. The prick on the finger didn't hurt as much as the humiliation of having to sell his blood. He thought about buying food with his blood money. This completed the cycle somehow. Next in the process was a procedure that can be compared to a jail booking. Identification, mug shots, and a medical history interview. The only thing missing was the fingerprinting.

The next room was a waiting room. After leaving a little cup of piss, Luke had another interview and a cursory physical exam. He then passed to the next room.

This was the bleeding room. The room was large and barnlike. Instead of cow stanchions, there were rows of green vinyl beds.

He watched a vampire wiping down the vinyl bed that was temporarily between plasma producers. He saw a plasma producer walking slowly off to collect his ten dollars. The whole place was a flurry of activity. The vampires were doing most of the moving around. The plasma producers were horizontal with the white-clad vampires hovering like bats around them.

Luke went in and laid down. He was mentally prepared for the bloodletting. The vampire cheerfully explained what she was doing as she was doing it. Not once did their eyes meet.

The needle was about the size of a sixty-penny nail. He felt two punctures as she pushed the needle in: one as the needle stretched and perforated the skin and the second as the needle perforated the vein. He noticed that the vinyl bed was still warm from the last occupant.

About this time, Luke's cousin came in. He laid down to be bled on the next bed. They told each other stories and gossiped the rest of the process away. The last Luke saw of his blood was when the vampire whisked the plastic bag away.

Luke left with ten dollars in his pocket. He had a bandage on his arm, and when he got outside, he saw the parking ticket on his car. He must have been hooked up to corporate America too long. The four-dollar ticket reduced his profit to six dollars.

While driving home, Luke saw his brother-in-law, Dave, at the drive-up window at the bank. This was the same Dave that owed him money from last fall. Luke had sold Dave a canoe.

Dave looked cashy as he left the bank. Luke followed him. When Dave pulled into a café, Luke followed him. Luke had coffee, and they entertained each other telling stories.

Luke's stories always centered around a canoe. Pretty soon Dave remembered that he still owed Luke for the canoe. He paid up.

When Luke got home, he checked the mail. As he was dividing the envelopes, he noticed one from an attorney. That one would stay in the pile of envelopes that had picture windows.

After reading the mail from his relatives, he began opening the picture-window envelopes. The one from the attorney had a letter, a release form, and a check. The check was for an accident that happened a couple of years ago. Luke could hardly remember the accident but knew it wasn't his fault.

The $1,700 check plus the $200, plus the $6 for his blood gave him a net profit of $1,906. Not bad for one day. He wondered how long this prosperity part of the cycle would last.

The first thing he bought was a box of Band-Aids for that hole in his arm.

wanna be

I ran into one last week.
I could tell he was a phony.
He didn't have the eyes.
Was he a door gunner or a lurp?
No, he was a green beret, river boat,
Seal, Ranger, Recon Marine.
I listened to his story,
He talked about the jungles, the
rice paddies, the firefights,
the weapons.
I listened.
He talked about mosquitoes,
snakes, gooks, and the NVA.
I listened until I realized we
had both seen the same Vietnam
war movie.
Nice try, fella
don't steal my war.

FRITZ AND BUTCH

"No shit, it was the vice president of the United States."

"Sure it was. And I suppose he brought the pope with him," said Dunkin Black Kettle.

"No, it was just him. He had all kinds of Secret Service guys with him," said Luke Warmwater. "See, I even got his autograph," he said as he handed his cousin a piece of paper with a signature scrawled on it.

"Yah, right. Anyone can write like this. You can't even make out what it says."

"It says Walter F. Mondale. See, right there. It's his name, right there in front of you, in black-and-white."

"Give me another piece of paper like this and I'll make you another autograph. What name do you want me to scribble?" asked Dunkin.

"Watch the TV news tonight. See if they talk about the vice president visiting Duluth today."

Luke and Dunkin were in the bar at the Radisson Hotel. A housing conference was being held there. Luke joined the Indians who were celebrating the end of the day's business.

Dunkin was making his moves on three women from White Earth Reservation. He'd called his cousin to come and help snag the three women. He'd also called another cousin, Butch Storyteller, to come join them.

As usual, Butch was late, so Dunkin and Luke were doing their best to entertain the three out-of-town visitors. Just as Dunkin was getting started on one of his best stories, a Secret Service guy came in the bar, gave it a professional once over, and stood by the door.

The Indians were curious now. "See, I told you," said Luke as the Indians watched to see what was going to happen. Walter Mondale and his entourage walked by the entrance to the bar and proceeded to the elevator.

"I'll be damned. I caught you telling the truth," said

Dunkin as he resumed his snagging. He wasn't getting very far because the conversation kept returning to the subject of the vice president.

Since they were talking about the vice president instead of vice, like Dunkin wanted, he put his snagging moves on hold. He figured he could use the vice president's visit to his advantage. The Indians drifted out to the hall to catch a glimpse of the vice president when he came back down in the elevator.

"I wonder if Butch got lost. He was supposed to be here a half hour ago," muttered Dunkin as he watched the White Earth women wander off.

"How could he get lost? He's lived around Dull Tooth all his life," answered Luke.

"He'd better get here pretty soon, or there'll be no reason to come down here."

"Ding," said the elevator as it opened and disgorged four Secret Service guys. They fanned out and checked the hall for possible danger. The Indians were all lined up along one wall, sipping their drinks, waiting for Fritz to make his appearance. The Secret Service was lined up on the other side of the hall, watching the Indians and the rest of the crowd gathering. The Indians talked, joked, and laughed as they waited.

About this time, the local TV crews arrived and set up their lights and cameras. They were going to tape the vice president as he walked by.

"I'll get his autograph for you," Dunkin told one of the White Earth women, as he resumed his snagging moves.

"Ding," said the elevator. The TV lights came on, the crowd collectively leaned forward, the Secret Service tensed up. All eyes were on the door, waiting for it to open.

The door opened, and Butch came strolling out. He was whistling a nameless tune. The lust in his eyes was replaced by fright as he saw the lights and all the people standing there looking at him. He was dressed in a Levi's jacket and was wearing a bone choker on his neck. The Indians recognized him right away. They were laughing and applauding.

"Speech, speech! Can you comment on your policy on Indian housing, Mr. Vice President?" the Indians asked Butch. Butch walked out about four steps, froze, then spun around and tried to get back in the elevator. He was there to snag, not meet the media or be escorted by the Secret Service. The doors closed in his face. He tried to pry them open with his fingers, but that didn't work. He faced the doors for a long three seconds and then finally turned around.

He recovered his composure and, in his best Richard Nixon impression ever, threw his anus in the air, made two peace signs with his fingers, shook his jowls, and said, "My fellow Americans." The TV lights were turned off.

"Ding," the elevator doors opened again and Fritz came out. He looked slightly confused as he saw the Indians gathered around Butch, laughing.

The TV lights came on again and Fritz walked through the crowd, shaking hands and smiling. He was also signing autographs. Dunkin went up to Fritz and got his signature on a piece of paper. It was the same piece of paper Luke had showed him earlier. Fritz smiled as he recognized his signature. He signed it again and gave it back to Dunkin.

"Anybody can get an autograph, I got you two of them," Dunkin told the White Earth woman. She put the paper in her purse, and they all went back to the bar. The White Earth women and the Fond du Lac men sat down and began to get to know each other.

"Let me tell you about the time the three of us jumped on a plane and went to a party in Wisconsin," said Dunkin as he gazed deep into the eyes of the woman he was sitting with.

"This isn't the first time this has happened to me. I think Fritz kind of looks like me," Butch told the woman he was sitting with.

Luke smiled. Life was back to normal.

war talk

Were you in the war?
yes
What was it like?
like nothing you can imagine
Did you kill anyone?
yes
How did that feel?
I felt like a murderer, a
savior, a cog in a machine
Did any of your friends get
killed?
yes
How did that feel?
Get the fuck out of my face!

THE ODYSSEY

Dunkin Black Kettle, Luke Warmwater, and Tom Skin were playing their usual game of finding work. They were out of employment and unemployment checks.

Just to pass the time, they were talking nostalgically about jobs they had in the past. TV was the only place they saw people working. They knew these things worked in cycles, but this last period of unwork was lasting too long.

Someone came by and told Dunkin he had a phone message. He went next door to his sister's house to use the phone. It was about a job.

"It's a one-day shot. Drive to St. Cloud, load up some furniture, and drive back. Twenty bucks each," said Dunkin.

"Not much job security there," Luke observed.

"It's twenty bucks more than you got now," Tom teased.

"What the hell, let's do it. You weren't doing anything this month, anyway," said Dunkin.

They bummed a ride over to look at the truck. The fifteen-thousand-pound monster looked like a bread truck or a SWAT team truck.

"Which is it?" Tom wanted to know.

"Depends. Do you want to eat or fight?" Luke deadpanned.

A pretrip inspection of the truck showed a frayed fan belt, a broken bolt on the coil, shorting plug wires, and an exhaust system that efficiently pumped fumes into the passenger part of the truck. The wipers worked. When one was going east, the other was going west.

It was one of those cold, misty, foggy mornings. The kind where you wish it would rain just to get it over with. The gray clouds covered the sky, sometimes all the way to the ground. It was good that the wipers worked.

They got a map, trip money, and a promise of more work. They got in and began the trip. Their first pit stop was three miles down the road. They stopped in Sawyer for jumper cables, a little food, coffee, and smokes.

Luke was driving because Tom's driver's license was sick and Dunkin's was dead.

As they started off, everyone became the navigator. Each one knew the best way to the freeway.

"I'll take the tar road to the freeway," said Luke.

"Three miles closer down the gravel road," said Tom.

"Highway patrol doesn't go down the gravel road," observed Dunkin.

They went down the gravel road.

As they drove along, different places brought out different stories.

"This is the corner Georgie bragged about. He said he could take it at fifty," Luke remembered.

"He was half right," Dunkin laughed.

"Yup, rolled it over exactly halfway through."

"Here's the field the state game wardens chased us from."

"Yah, we got away clean that time."

"They could stay with us on the straightaways, but we lost them on the corners."

"Dunkin was really wheeling that night."

"He shut off the lights and passed that car waiting to enter the highway."

"The game wardens followed that guy. I think they got him stopped down by the Big Lake Road."

They laughed together as they invented conversations between the driver and the game wardens. They remembered the twenty-five-year-old chase as if it happened last week. By the time they were finished with that story, they were at the freeway.

They began to play like real truckers.

"10-4, back door," said Luke as he spoke into his imaginary CB mike.

He slid in behind a semi on the freeway.

As the men rode along, they admired a bridge that Dunkin had worked on a couple summers before. He told that story for a good five miles past the bridge.

It was blue inside the truck from the exhaust, but after experimenting with the windows and doors, they were able to make the air breathable.

The monotony of the trip was broken up by more stories. By the time they got to St. Cloud, the back of the truck was full of them and their embellished outcomes.

There was a pile of guys in one corner, all knocked out with one punch.

There were seven deer in another corner, all killed with one shot from five hundred yards away.

There were at least seven hundred pounds of wild rice, all knocked in one day.

The fish were so big their tails were sticking out the back of the truck.

There almost wasn't room for the pile of ducks, all shot at impossible distances.

There was at least a year of jail time in the back of the truck. There were overnighters, some thirties, and a couple of nineties.

The back of the truck contained four dogs that could dive deeper, come up drier, and outretrieve any other dog in town.

There was a parking lot full of great cars of the past. A '51 Ford, a '69 Chevy, a '75 Ford pickup.

There were so many stones in the back of the truck they had to stop for gas. They were in St. Cloud.

After gas, they drove to the *X* on the map. They found the place right away. The furniture wasn't too heavy. They loaded the truck, and when Dunkin slammed the back door, it fell off.

He picked it up and threw it in with the furniture.

It was beginning to sprinkle as they left town. They found the right road and began to trek home.

The towns crawled by. It was starting to get dark. By the time they got to Moose Lake, it was completely dark. The rain was heavier too.

None of the three Sawyer Indians knew it, but the fan belt was dying. It had stretched about six inches and was occasionally turning the fan.

The engine got hot—so hot it started a fire in the engine compartment. The steam escaped from the radiator and drowned the wiring. The steam did not put out the fire.

The smoking, steaming truck coasted off at the Mahtowa exit. They all gave orders.

"Get the fire extinguisher."

"Stop the truck."

"Open the hood."

"Find some water."

The truck stopped, the hood opened, the fire was put out.

They found some water in the ditch and cooled the engine. They dried the wires and were back on the road again, wondering how far they could make it without a fan belt.

The hot engine made them stop wondering about three miles down the road.

The first time, it was just a standard roadside emergency—stop the truck, put out the fire, cool the radiator. This second emergency happened right by Otter Creek, so they had no trouble cooling the radiator.

The trouble came when Luke tried to start the truck. The same belt also charges the battery, he thought.

Tom flagged down a passing motorist. The good Samaritan gave them a jump, and they were on their way again.

They made a dramatic, smoking, steaming entrance at the truck stop on Highway 210. They were seven miles from home and the trip was over. Dunkin called the owner of the truck and told him what was happening. The owner asked if the fire was out. Dunkin assured him it was.

He came to the truck stop, paid them for their labors, and gave them a ride to Sawyer. He felt so bad about the truck and the trip, he offered them a three-week job.

Dunkin Black Kettle, Luke Warmwater, and Tom Skin had found work again.

tipi reflections

I moved into a tipi
my friends think I'm strange.
My family thinks I'm nuts.
Both friends and family wish
they were strange and nuts
enough to do it also.
The design is thousands of
years of a man wondering
will this work?

Candles, an old design also,
seem best for lighting the tipi
and your inner sense of beauty.

The canvas is strong enough
to stop the north wind
yet delicate enough to cast
shadows from the cooking fire.

Grandpa called it *bajeeshkaogan*
and knew all about it
before I was born
the poles, rising up and
carrying your eyes, thoughts,
and prayers to the sky and beyond

the door opening, too low to
catch the morning sun, watches
the smoke flaps catch and spread
the message of another miracle,
another morning.

The tipi contained people
sitting around a fire eating
freshly roasted meat
it could have been yesterday
or eons ago.

The tipi also contained a small
boy, excited by the duty of
tending the fire, staring at the
flames for hours
making good childhood memories

for fun, telling your misbehaving
children they will soon have to
go stand in the corner

visitors, sleeping in a circle
looking like wagon wheel spokes
the fire—the hub.

The smell of wood smoke
clings to me when I have to
go to the city, it is a
reminder of where I come from
and where I'm going.

Meanwhile, the loons sing to
me and get just as excited
when the bald eagle flies
although for different reasons.

Through the smoke opening at
night I see the stars
by day I see the clouds
and sky.

The idea of living in a tipi
is so unusual it always brings
out the "what you should do is"
in people who visit.

How many men have stood where
I stand, thinking what a
fine place to live?

HOLIDAY INNDIANS

Luke Warmwater and his cousin were on the road. Butch Storyteller was driving his car. It was a good car: the radio and heater both worked. They had spent the previous day preparing the car for the trip. The problems of gas, oil, and tires had been solved. Luke hocked one of his shotguns to buy a tire.

The two Sawyer skins were on their way to Minneapolis. The National Indian Education Convention was being held at one of the hotels there. Since they were both college students, they were mildly interested in Indian education. They were more interested in the fancy snagging that went on at these conventions.

Indians from all over the United States would be there. Luke and Butch were interested in meeting Indians of the female gender. The two skins would become members of the Holiday Inndian tribe for the duration of the convention.

To quote the novelist Snoopy, "It was a dark and stormy night." The snow started before they got to the sweet rolls at Hinckley, Minnesota. In the headlights, the snow seemed to be coming from a point about twenty feet in front of the car. The snow was the kind that fell in a horizontal direction.

As usual, they were late getting started. Because of the snow, they had to slow all the way down to the speed limit. This made them late for the opening of the convention. Butch said, "When I die, they're going to call me the late Butch Storyteller."

Luke laughed and said, "Who did you steal that line from?"

Butch started telling about the snagging he did at the last funeral in Sawyer. "That woman I met there was so pretty she would have made Miss Indian America look like a boy—an ugly boy."

"She might have been with you, Butch, but she was thinking of me all the time," said Luke.

"Yeah, but whose relative was that I saw you with? I thought you told me she was a good one—you said she wanted to marry you."

"She might have been thirty or forty pounds heavier than I first thought and maybe ten, fifteen years older when I first saw her in the good light," Luke added defensively.

They laughed and lied their way down the slippery interstate to the Cities. The anticipation started to build as they got closer to the Cities. They took turns telling convention stories. Butch fondly remembered the one in Milwaukee.

"There were eleven floors of partying Indians in that sixteen-floor hotel. One guy told me he wound up eight floors away from where he registered."

"That was me, don't you remember? I fell in lust with that woman from Tama, Iowa. We would be living together today if her big boyfriend from Arizona hadn't shown up. I'm glad he didn't want to fight me," Luke remembered.

"Sipping, snagging, and silliness went on for four days at that one, as I recall," Butch said.

"Uh huh, don't forget the nights either."

"How could I?"

The last big convention that Butch and Luke had attended was in Denver. It was a library-related convention. "Remember that librarian I met there?" Butch asked.

"She was from Wisconsin, wasn't she?"

"Yeah, she showed me what the last syllable in Wisconsin really means."

"How about the woman I was with? She was from Washington, DC. She explained the Library of Congress classification system to me as we explored each other's systems."

"Do you ever hear from her anymore?"

"I get a postcard now and then."

"Maybe you'll get lucky and see her at this convention."

"Who knows?"

With the memories of that convention still tickling them, they arrived at the hotel. They were late. The evening proceedings were all over with. The snagging was pretty well done by the time they arrived. The bars and restaurants were all closed.

Butch and Luke decided to hang around the lobby to see if anyone else had arrived late. The elevator door quietly opened behind the two skins from the Fond du Lac reservation. They heard it and turned to see who was getting off.

Two women got off. One of them was thin and the other was quite large. As the two women prowled the lobby, Butch observed, "They look like the number ten when they walk together like that."

The women circled around and came up to the two Sawyer skins. The women were out snagging. Butch and Luke became the snagees instead of the snaggers.

Before they really knew what was happening, Butch and Luke found themselves in the women's hotel room. Everyone introduced themselves.

"I'm Patty, and I'm from Turtle Mountain," said the thin one. Butch thought she was built like a rice knocker.

"I'm June, and I'm from Turtle Mountain too." Butch thought she was so big she could be called June, July, and part of August.

Butch said, "I'm George, and I'm a Seneca from New York."

"I'm Frank, and I live in Ohio. I'm a Winnebago," Luke lied.

Trying to make the best of the situation, Butch and Luke sat down and tried to drink the women pretty. Luke suspected the two were trying to drink them handsome. It later turned out there was not enough beer in the room or even in the whole building. Everyone in the room told their life stories as they settled into the drinking party. Butch and Luke continued telling lies.

Patty got up and looked out the window. She wondered aloud, "I wonder what I'd look like if I fell out of this window?"

"You'd look like hamburger, Patty," June told her.

They were out of beer. Butch quit telling funny stories

because every time he did June would laugh and punch him on the arm. His arm was getting sore. Patty's response to Butch's stories was to laugh and stick out her tongue almost to her chin and say "Haaaaaaaa."

It looked like June was trying to edge Butch over to a corner. He was trying to keep a lane open to the door. She outweighed him by fifty pounds, and he was getting worried.

Butch eased over toward the door, invented an emergency, then left the room to move his car, make a phone call, or something. Luke hung around the room for a few minutes and then left to go check on his cousin.

They weren't drunk enough to wake up any of their relatives at this ungodly hour, so they found a cheap hotel and slept. Tomorrow was the second day of the four-day convention.

end of the beginning

Someone said we begin to die
the minute we're born.
Death is a part of life.
Who knows why the Creator
thins the herd.
Another old saying says
we must all be prepared
to give up those we love
or die first.
Take time to mourn.
Take time to remember.
Everything happens in cycles.
The pain you feel was once
balanced by someone's joy
when that baby was born.
The loss you feel today
will be replaced by good
long-lasting memories.
Is there a message here? Yah,
treat others like this
is your last day above ground.

COFFEE DONUTS

The semitrailer trucks roared down the highway on this, a rainy October morning. The car waiting to enter the highway was rocked by the wind and washed by the spray as the loaded grain trucks went by.

The three skins from the Fond du Lac reservation didn't mind the wait. It was raining, and they didn't have to go to work. This meant they had nowhere to go and a long time to get there.

The driver was bragging about his car and was giving the boys a demonstration ride through the ditchbanks. The driver had just bought the car and paid the insurance with his earnings from the job at the reservation housing project.

It was a pretty good car, and it looked like it would last through two winters. The tires were good, the lights worked, the radio was loud, and the heater blew hot; hell, even the cigarette lighter worked.

The job at the housing project added stability to the driver's life. The Friday paychecks seemed to mellow out his old lady, and she didn't seem as snaky as before when they were on welfare. Since he wasn't drinking anymore, the driver spent more time with his kids instead of hanging out at the local tavern. Because of the size of his family, he was next on the list to get one of those new houses they were building. He was thinking these things as he slid sideways around the corner on the empty gravel road.

As he was bragging how well the car held the road, the passenger in the middle slid into the guy riding shotgun. The passenger in the middle was just happy to be riding. He was happy to be out.

He had spent the past year in and out of jails and treatment centers. His troubles had begun last year over an open bottle charge. Instead of jail and a fine, he chose to pay his debt to society by going to a treatment center for chemical abusers. After a few hours in the facility, he left. This meant the law was looking for him. After a few months of freedom, he was caught and had to go back and do his time in the county jail.

Finally, it was all behind him on this, his second day of real freedom. He had been told to report for work the next day at the housing project.

The passenger in the middle knew of a pickup truck he could get cheap. He could drop in the engine from his old car and fix that truck up pretty good now that he was going to be cashy. He was explaining how to hook up the transmission as they slid around another corner. As he slid on the seat, his elbow dug into the shotgun's rib.

The elbow in the rib brought the shotgun back into the conversation. The shotgun had been looking at the edge of a field for a deer. True to his name, the guy riding shotgun had a shotgun. The rusty, trusty twelve-gauge was deer hungry.

When riding with Shotgun, it was hard to talk to him 'cause all you could see as the back of his head as he looked for deer.

Shotgun was happy 'cause he was working. He was happy about the job at the housing project. The job paid for a new deer rifle and a canoe. He was happy he didn't have to work today so he could go hunting.

He remembered giving the driver a similar ride a couple weeks ago when he got his new truck. Shotgun's new truck was a four-wheeler, and it allowed him to go deeper into the brush before getting stuck.

The driver chuckled as he remembered how long it took to dig the truck out of that last swamp. The driver thought *Enough of this crazy driving* as they approached the state highway and civilization again. As the three skins entered the state highway, they began to argue about where to go next. The driver wanted to go home and take his old lady and kids shopping. He also wanted to continue the riding and hunting.

The passenger didn't care. He was just happy to be out

and riding. The shotgun wanted to go get his truck and continue the riding and hunting.

The driver was adjusting the rearview mirror. The passenger was digging under the seat for his stolen jailhouse copy of O. Henry stories. The shotgun was again looking for deer.

They didn't see the grain truck with the sleeping driver coming at them in their lane.

ditched

A first grader
A federal boarding school
Pipestone
Said anin to the
first grown up
Got an icy blue-eyed stare
in return
Got a beating from a
second grader for crying
about the stare
Couldn't tell ma or dad
both were 300 miles away
Couldn't write, didn't know how
Couldn't mail, didn't know how
Ran away, got caught
Got an icy blue stare
and a beating
Got another beating
from a second grader
for crying about
the blue-eyed beating
Institutionalized
Toughed it out
Survived

THE YELLOW HAND CLAN

"Wake up. I don't care if you got a hangover; they're hiring right now. I just heard about it," said Rod Grease as he tried to wake his friend Luke Warmwater.

"C'mon let's get over there before some light-skinned Indian gets the job," Rod continued.

"They always hire them wannabe Indians anyway," said Luke as he tried to recapture his nap.

"No, this time they got an Indian doing the hiring. I guess all the white guys were busy."

"Okay, okay, I'll get up."

"Hurry up then. My car is still idling and I'm low on gas," Rod told him.

"We gotta find some of those yellow gloves so it looks like we're serious about working," said Luke as he sat up and put on his work boots.

A few minutes later, Luke came out of the bathroom. "All right, I'm ready," he said. "I wish I didn't have that one beer last night."

"One beer?"

"Yah, it was the twenty-eighth or twenty-ninth one that gave me this hangover. Look over here, Rod; is my head still on my shoulders?"

"Uh huh, it's still there. You do look pretty rough, though. Maybe they'll hire you 'cause you look so desperate."

"What kind of jobs are open? I haven't been a carpenter in quite a while."

"The wannabe Indians got all the easy jobs. The only ones left are on the block crew, building basements," Rod told him.

"I never done that before. Can't be too hard to learn."

"Not hard to learn, hard to keep doing. Them blocks weigh forty-five pounds each," said Rod as he threw his car in gear. He headed toward the job site.

"My new old lady packed me a lunch," Rod bragged.

"If we get on that crew, we can cancel the weightlifting class," joked Luke as he finished lacing up his boots.

"I can handle it. I lift a heavy weight every morning when I get up to piss," laughed Rod.

"I think you're bragging," Luke told him.

"Maybe a little bit," Rod admitted.

They got to the job site. The Fond du Lac Reservation had signed a contract to build two hundred HUD houses. The federal job was paying the union wage.

While walking across, they met Cliff Spinaway. He was the Indian doing the hiring.

"We're here to work; we're both good workers," Luke told Cliff.

"We've done this kind of work before," Rod lied.

"We're dependable, we don't lie, cheat, or steal, we respect motherhood, we salute the flag, we're kind to puppies, and Rod here is so strong he has muscles in his shit," Luke lied.

"Okay, you're both hired," Cliff laughed. He hired them just to shut them up; he was almost starting to believe them. Them Sawyer Indians sure are mouthy, he thought.

While driving away, Cliff laughed to himself. He knew the backbreaking work the two guys had talked themselves into.

Rod and Luke joined the yellow hand clan. They were laborers but were officially called mason tenders.

They walked over to the hole in the ground. Louie Wise Owl from Sawyer was mixing mud, the gray in-between stuff that holds the blocks together.

"I heard about this before you guys. I got the easy job," Louie teased.

"You two guys carry the blocks, I mix the mud and deliver it with the wheelbarrow." Louie recited the mixture: "Nine shovels of sand, one bag of mortar, water, and another nine shovels of sand, mix it until it shakes like a fat lady's ass." Louie pointed out the blocks Rod and Luke were to carry.

Both grabbed a block in each hand and carried them to

where the masons were laying the wall up. They were new on the job and were kept running. They hadn't worked for a while and were out of shape.

"Blocks," the masons would yell. Rod and Luke ran with blocks to meet this new crisis—a mason without blocks to lay.

"This is nothing but bull labor. Why did you wake me up?" Luke asked.

"You're getting union wages, so quit crying," Rod told him.

"On this job, you don't need brains, only a strong back."

"Yup, strong like bull, smart like tractor," Rod added.

Louie went by, whistling a nameless tune, pushing a wheelbarrow of mud.

"How come he's always pushing that wheelbarrow?" asked Rod.

"Didja ever try pulling one?" answered Luke.

"No, I mean why don't one of us have that easy job?"

"Louie got here five minutes before us, and he mixed mud on another job before."

"Blocks, we need blocks over here," yelled a mason, putting an end to their conversation. There is nothing tender about being a mason tender, Luke thought.

After the next thirty basements, they got good at the job. They could haul enough blocks to keep the masons busy all morning. Then they could stand around, leaning on a shovel, watching the masons and the mud mixer working.

Part of Louie's job was to wheel the mud down into the hole. He used an eight inch, fourteen foot plank. For the first half, he was in control of the heavy wheelbarrow. For the second half of the trip, he was just along for the ride. At the bottom, he would dig his feet in, plowing furrows with the wheelbarrow until it stopped. It was a controlled crash.

One afternoon they watched Louie make one of his now famous runs down the plank. He didn't know it but the plank was split. Louie found out about halfway down. He and the loaded wheelbarrow went off the plank sideways.

The wheelbarrow broke three blocks, and Louie took out three more with his shoulder. He laid there, crumpled up.

"Get up, no laying down on this job," yelled Rod.

"You're going to have to pay for those blocks," Luke teased.

Rod and Luke went over and picked Louie up. He checked himself out and decided he was still good for fifteen rounds.

The hot summer dragged on, basement by basement. One day, Luke made the startling calculation that they had worked long enough for unemployment compensation. Rocking chair money all winter.

"I think my old lady is mad at me," said Rod one day when they sat down to eat lunch.

"Yah?" said Luke as he poured coffee. He dug out a baloney-and-commodity-cheese sandwich.

"Let's trade sandwiches," said Rod as he sipped his coffee.

"What makes you think that, Rod?" said Luke as he passed his sandwich over.

"She's been acting strange lately, almost like she's making leaving noises," Rod explained.

Luke took a big bite out of the sandwich he got from Rod. He spit it out even faster. There was something wrong with it. He peeked inside the bread and discovered it was a dry-oatmeal-and-mustard sandwich. Rod checked the other things in his lunch. One was a dry-cornmeal-and-ketchup sandwich. Another baggie had what looked like dried-out fry bread dough.

"I don't think she loves you anymore, Rod," Luke advised.

Sure enough, when Rod got home from work, she was gone, and so were all her clothes.

"I guess the union wages didn't impress her anymore," said Luke when he heard about it.

Rod spent the rest of the summer finding someone who was impressed with his union wages. He found three or four someones.

The two Sawyer Indians were standing around, leaning on their shovels. They saw Cliff Spinaway drive up. They got busy real quick.

They didn't fool Cliff. He had worked construction a long time. He laughed as he got out of his pickup truck. Cliff knew these two guys were good workers, but winter was coming.

"Sorry boys, I gotta lay you off until next spring."

"Does this mean we have to stay home, laying around, collecting unemployment checks?" asked Rod.

"Yup. Go down to the Unemployment Office and sign up."

"Okay," they said in unison. They grinned all the way to town. Rod now had plenty of time to find someone who was impressed with a steady income all winter.

weegwas

Time to gather bark,
another gift from the Creator.
Just doing what grandpa did
like his grandpa before him.
Went with a cousin I've known
since we ate oatmeal
from the same bowl.
Mosquitoes and deer flies
welcomed us to their feast.
A sparrow hawk flew by,
supper in his feet.
Watched a deer feeding
in the lake shallows.
Each tree leads to others
farther from the road,
found one that's been
waiting sixty years
to become a basket.
A cut allows the bark
to crack crack open
hands slipped inside
feel the smooth wet
the bark jumps from the tree
eager to help us
make a basket or two.
Finally we have enough bark
it was time to go home
we were getting hungry.

YOUR STANDARD DRUNK

Luke and his cousin Dunkin were on a dirty drunk.

"Have a beer," said Luke one fine summer morning.

"How long we been doing this now?"

"About three weeks, I think," said Luke.

They were drinking at Dunkin's house at Perch Lake. It was far enough in the woods that cops didn't visit. It wasn't too far for people who wanted to drink. It was a mecca for the drinkers in the community. It also was like a magnet for runaway wives, husbands, and children. This was a good drunk. No one went to jail or the hospital.

Luke and Dunkin had many visitors during their drunk. Some came to drink, some came to talk, and all came to eat. The visitors brought food and more to drink. Whatever was needed to continue the drunk was carried in by the next visitor.

During the day, they drank by the lake; at night, they drank by campfire.

Jack Sky came to drink and talk. He told his favorite story, his life story.

"Damn right, I'm Ottawa and proud of it. I've lived around here longer than most of you," said Jack.

Jack came to the reservation when he was a little guy. He grew up and married a local woman. He now had children and grandchildren living all over the rez.

"Just when I think I belong here, someone makes a smartass remark about Ottawa Indians," Jack complained. "I've lived here for forty years, but someone has to remind me I'm not really from here," said Jack as he took a long pull from his bottle.

The story was good enough to get him drunk and fed many times. He was getting kind of old, so he was only good for a week and four tellings of his life story.

Another one of the visitors was a young girl. She told her life story, which didn't take too long. "My ma is mean, she won't get me a phone or color TV for my bedroom. I showed her—I took off," said the young girl as she began her crying jag.

Dunkin handed Luke a beer and said, "Remember what it was like when we were kids?"

"Yah, sleeping four to a bed with the snow blowing through the cracks and piling up on the blankets."

"How about hauling water in a cream can, on a sled in the winter and a wagon in the summer."

"Yah, I sure hated the days when my ma washed clothes."

"All she's got to worry about is a phone and a TV."

The people sitting around began to laugh and tease her.

"I want a color TV," begged an old man in a falsetto voice.

"I want a phone in my bedroom," giggled an older woman.

As the teasing went on, the young girl was looking for a way out of the teasing. Her mother drove up and grabbed her. She threw the young girl in the car and threw threats around about allowing kids at parties like this one.

Luke handed Dunkin a beer as they watched them drive away.

"Some parents wouldn't come after their kids," said Luke.

"Uh huh, some kids wouldn't come after their parents either," agreed Dunkin.

Wild Man showed up one day. "I was down in the Cities when I heard about this drunk," he said. "No one came into the Corral Bar and offered me a job so I came home.

"Look who I invited," Wild Man said as he went to the back of his truck. In the back of the truck was a deer.

The deer was a fat juicy one and was skinned and cleaned immediately. Wild Man gave the younger ones a lesson in skinning and cleaning a deer. He also told them where he shot it and how he offered the deer spirit some tobacco.

When Wild Man kicked back and opened a beer, someone else began the cutting and cooking. It wasn't too long after that everyone was eating. There was grease from ears to elbows. The drinking and eating continued on through the night.

The next morning they heard a big truck rumbling up. It was a beer truck. A couple of Luke's cousins got out when it stopped. They went around and helped the driver out. He was a white man.

"We were drinking with this white guy last night."

"He said he wanted to come out here and drink with Indians."

The white guy looked like he was ready to pass out. He looked around and said, "I've got a lot of Indian friends. Help yourself to some beer." He sat down and then fell over sideways and began snoring. Whenever he'd wake up, someone would hand him a beer or a shot of whiskey. He'd take a drink and then pass out again.

Luke thought this was too much good luck. This much good luck would also bring an equal amount of bad luck, not to mention the cops.

Luke and Dunkin passed out a couple of twelve-packs and loaded the driver back into his truck. They wrote out an IOU and a thank-you note. They pinned the notes on the driver and locked the truck.

On the way back home, they decided the drunk was about over.

"Let's send everyone home when we run out of beer."

"Yah, time to get ready for ricing anyway."

Both of them were dreading the three weeks worth of hangover they had coming.

lifetime of sad

She's fifty, alone, and drunk.
She has pride in her language
but no one to talk to.
Some don't understand.
Some can't, some won't.
She's buried two husbands,
warriors in the white man's wars.
Her children are raised and gone,
a five-year battle with cancer,
a longer battle with the bottle.
She's broke and fifty miles from her empty bed
alcohol failed her, she's too
drunk to talk, but not drunk
enough to pass out.
Her eyes show a lifetime of sad.
She cried out for beer, smokes,
attention, or affection.
She only got the attention.
When she was caught stealing
food from the house she was visiting
she was asked to leave.
She left fifty, alone, and drunk.

THE JAIL TRAIL

The commodity cans were melting through the snow when Luke Warmwater went to jail this time. It wasn't his first time in the barrel. He knew all the jailers by name and disposition. He was disgusted to be in jail and was also disgusted that the whole routine was so familiar to him.

The jailer who let him in was friendly as he booked him. He even greeted him by name. The poor bastard, Luke thought, he's been doing his time, eight hours at a time since the last time. Life in jail on the installment plan.

Empty pockets, a shower, and a clean green jail jumpsuit completed the metamorphosis of the free Sawyer Indian to a number. He did remember to ask for a large jumpsuit. It wouldn't bind in the long hours coming. He also asked for an extra blanket because the pillows in this jail were always small.

He wondered who he would know in the cell block. There were always Indians in jail. He also thought no more food worries. He had to catch himself. He almost thanked the jailer who opened, held, and then locked the steel door behind him.

He looked for an empty bunk to claim as his space. He spotted one the same time he spotted his cousin Dunkin Black Kettle.

His cousin quit the solitaire card game he was playing and began to deal a cribbage hand for Luke. All right, thought Luke. He adjusted to jail immediately. While Luke and his cousin played cards, they caught up on each other's life and crimes.

Getting used to jail did take some time, though. That was okay because Luke had nothing but time. Sleeping in the same large room with mostly strangers, mostly criminals, was a shock at first. After listening to these strangers belch, moan, snore, and talk in their sleep, they didn't stay strangers long. Some did remain criminals, though.

Jail quickly settled into a routine. Eat, sleep, play cards, watch TV. It went on and on. Eat, sleep, play cards, watch TV. *Incarceration* was too nice-sounding a word to describe their plight.

One of the guys in the cell block would begin each day by sighing. There were heavy sighs, laughing sighs, and sighs of all sizes. Luke got to know everyone's habits in no time.

After conferring with his jailhouse lawyers, the other prisoners, Luke decided that treatment at a chemical abusers place was the way out of his current predicament. Abusing whiskey had gotten him in jail; he wanted to see if it would get him out. The jailhouse lawyers had all been through the mill and knew the drill.

Luke began the steps that would lead to the twelve steps at the treatment place. The last untreated Sawyer Indian was going down. He did get out of jail.

Just about everyone else of treatable age had been through one of the facilities. Some relatives from Sawyer had counted coup thirteen or more times.

There was one story going around that the state hospital was going to rename one wing of their facility. They were going to rename it for one of Luke's uncles because he had been there so many times. Luke thought the story was slightly exaggerated because he had another uncle who had been there just as many times. They were not going to name anything for him. The story was good for a chuckle, though.

He walked through the door of the treatment place. He was supposed to report in sometime in the morning. He walked in at one minute to noon. No sense rushing things, he thought.

Strangers, look at all the strangers. There must be at least fifty white people wandering around that he didn't know. Culture shock! Wait a second, on the other side of the room was a skin he recognized from the rez. It was a woman he was in jail with. She must have used the same trail to get out of jail. He threw her a Sawyer wave, and she smiled a greeting back. Good, another skin. He adjusted to treatment immediately.

Food. Luke saw food he hadn't seen in quite a while. So much of it too. As he shoveled the food in, Luke wondered if a guy could go back for thirds or even fourths. He didn't have to buy it, fry it, or clean up after it. Luke thought he was in food heaven.

Treatment. Generally what it consisted of was sitting around and talking about memorable drunks. During these soul-searching, guilt-provoking sessions, if one could work up a good cry the story was accepted as a true revelation. Whimpering along was not enough. It had to be wailing, gnashing of teeth, and heaving sobs. Certain rooms were designated as crying rooms. Luke could tell which ones they were; they had strategically placed Kleenex boxes.

Since he had quit crying for good in the fourth grade, Luke was at a slight disadvantage. He couldn't get extra points or credibility for tears. He did have some good drunk stories though.

Since he was a storyteller, he was ahead of the others in the "group grope" sessions. His stories were memorable and repeated throughout the facility. So much for confidentiality; you can't hold a good story down, he thought.

Anything that was said or unsaid, done or undone, was a symptom of the problem that brought a person to the facility, Luke quickly learned. He thought, if the only tool you have is a hammer, everything begins to look like a nail. That was the feeling of the place.

Guts. The whole place seemed to operate on guts. If you were not spilling your guts on the floor, you were not trying hard enough. He wondered if the people working there ever got tired of wading through human guts.

After getting the skinny from the other skin about how to get along, Luke began to live the role of the drying-out drunk. The other skin, who shall remain nameless because of the confidentiality rule, helped him along in the treatment place.

One day, when it was her turn to raise the flag, Luke helped her. Since it was a treatment place, they solemnly placed their hands over their livers as they raised the flag.

After successfully going through the phases of the program, Luke found himself ready to graduate out into the real world. He wondered how many of these strangers he'd know in three months. He wondered if he'd ever drink again. He wondered if the place did him any good. He didn't have to wonder if he was free. He knew he was. He was an ex-jailbird, spun-dry Sawyer Indian.

where you from?

Rice poles hold up clotheslines in Sawyer.
Rabbit chokers live there.
Wind in the trees and time to wonder
what makes that sound.
Time itself is measured by the sun
not quartz on the wrist.
In Sawyer, one knows the name of every dog in town
Nayquab, Johnson, Duke, King, Pal
and a lot of them named Puppy.
A Sawyer Shinnob knows the most devious, roundabout,
circular cop-free road to town when
the insurance is lapsed
the driver's license is sick
and the license plates are dead.
The mosquitoes are as big as eagles
and as common as leaves.

We're glad they haven't discovered
snowmobile suits or thermal underwear.
Teasing means I care, not that I want to hurt you.
In Sawyer, one can be mad at a brother or sister
and still have enough family.
Gossip is more common than surplus commodity food,
people walk on trails, not sidewalks,
getting longed by a short guy is unfortunate.
Hocking a satellite dish for bingo
is possible but difficult.
In Sawyer, generations of relatives are buried
the air hasn't been breathed by heavy industry
the colors of blue and green rest the eyes and spirits
the quiet makes it easy to hear the spirits
and their messages.
In Sawyer, the values and traditions of the people are held
sacred.

RICING AGAIN

Luke Warmwater woke up wondering where he was. He remembered being at the party and remembered being one of the last ones awake. It all came crashing back. He was at Mukwa's house, and he was supposed to meet that woman who was his new rice partner.

His head hurt, and he knew his breath was foul. His ribs hurt, and he wondered if he had been in a fight. No, no one had punched him. It must have been the way he slept. The couch was responsible for the rib ache. The alcohol was responsible for his parched throat, queasy stomach, and shaking fingers. The headache came from the guilt and the excessive amount of alcohol he had drunk.

His bloodshot eyes scanned the room looking for something to put out the fire in his throat and settle his stomach. He knew the guilt feeling would go away on its own. He saw a twelve-pack that had been overlooked last night. The twelver still had seven cold ones left. The world didn't look so bad now.

His old car was outside, and the cold beer in his belly was making him forget his assorted aches. He drained the bottle as he stood outside and drained his bladder.

The canoe was still on the car, and under a quilt in the backseat was his new partner, Dolly. She looked a little tough as she snored away her share of the party.

Dolly came from the other side of the rez. He knew he wasn't related to her, but had heard of her family. He also remembered her laugh from last night as she playfully punched him on the arm. He was trying to tell her how pretty she was when the punch stopped the chain of compliments. He looked forward to getting to know her better as soon as they straightened up a bit. As he was trying to remember everything he knew about her, he decided it wasn't important. What was important was to make rice.

Today was the first day of the opening of the "committee" lakes. Luke had a car, canoe, blockers, pole, and a new partner. He only had to find lunch and sacks for the green rice. They were signed up for Dead Fish Lake, and he didn't want to miss that first run through the ripe, untouched rice.

As he drove to the store to score the sacks and lunch, Dolly woke up and asked for a smoke. His crushed pack still had some left. As they lit up he thought, she really is pretty. He shared his beer with her as she began to pull herself together. She took his rearview mirror to comb her hair, inspect her teeth, cough, and blow her nose. She could complete her toilet at the bathroom in the store.

His headache was subsiding down to a dull throb as they pulled into the store parking lot. He saw a couple of cars he recognized and his cousin's truck. He reached for his wallet and suddenly realized he had been jackrolled as he slept on the couch. There must have been someone still awake when he went to sleep.

Dolly handed him his worn wallet and winked. She said she took it to protect his bankroll. He was beginning to like this woman more and more. His eleven dollars were still there.

For the car, Luke bought gas and a quart of oil and added air to that right rear tire that had a slow leak. For themselves, he got lunch materials and smokes. The store owner gave him a couple of sacks because he promised to sell his rice there.

As he drove to the lake, memories of past ricing seasons came to him. His earliest memories were of playing on the shore while his parents were out ricing. He knew the people enjoyed ricing and there were good feelings all around. Years seemed to melt from people. Grandparents moved about with a light step and without their canes. Laughing and loud talking broke out frequently. The cool crisp morning air and the smell of wood smoke, roasting meat, and coffee were all part of these early childhood memories.

When he grew older, his responsibilities increased. He

took care of his brothers and sisters. He cleaned the canoes and rice boats of every last kernel of rice. He learned how to make rice poles and knockers. He learned how important ricing was to the people.

His thoughts were jolted back to the present when his left rear tire blew out. He thought, Gee, that was my good tire too. As the car lurched to a stop, he knew he didn't have a spare 'cause he hocked it last week. He took the offending tire off because he knew he'd have to eventually. He looked down the road.

He saw one of his uncles coming down toward the rice landing. When his uncle saw what was wrong, he stopped and opened his trunk. He had a snow tire that still had some air. Luke shared a smoke and a beer with his uncle as he put the good tire on. As they sipped and gossiped, Luke found out that his uncle was not planning on ricing this year but was just going down to the landing to see if anyone needed a partner. His uncle was known as a good knocker so finding a partner was not going to be a problem.

The tire change made them late, and they had to park way back on the road. The canoe and all their stuff had to be packed a long way to the lake. Everyone else was lined up and ready to go.

The ricers laughed as Luke was getting in the water because his face showed what he'd been doing the night before. In the face of all this teasing, he could hardly wait for the jokes and jibes to be aimed at someone else so he could join in the laughter. It was good to see his relatives, anyway.

Dolly was standing in front of the canoe with her pole as he arranged his sacks, water jug, and—oops, must have left the lunch in the car. They drifted out to where the eager ones were waiting to blast off. Luke was knocking because this was his partner's first year ricing. He had looked at the rice while hunting and knew where on the lake to go.

He repeated the string of instructions to Dolly as they began. "Don't break the rice, stay out of the open water, keep the canoe moving, watch for the color of the ripe rice, if you feel yourself falling jump in and save the rice in the canoe."

Dolly looked comfortable in the front of the canoe, and they didn't feel tippy as they started off. She poled to the rice. The sound of the other ricers swishing through the rice made a nice rhythm. Luke chuckled when he heard the unmistakable sound of a knocker hitting a canoe instead of the rice. While loosening up his arm and shoulder muscles, he saw the heavy heads were hanging at just the right angle for easy knocking. The sound of the rice falling in the canoe made Luke feel good.

Everywhere he looked, there was good rice. This patch went all the way across the lake. A bald eagle circled above them. He interpreted this as a good sign.

After a couple hours, Luke's stomach reminded him of the lunch in the car. The rice had bearded up pretty good and was clean and free of debris. Not too shabby, thought Luke.

They stopped to visit with his first cousin who had stopped for lunch. The fry bread, deer meat, and green tea gave Luke and Dolly enough strength to finish the day. Luke thought he'd bring his cousin some of the next deer he shot.

After getting off the lake, they sacked up on the shore. Both Luke and Dolly joined in on the laughing and exaggerating as people told stories about what happened on the lake that day. The harvest was good, and everyone was happy with the way the rice was falling—except for the greedy ones, who wouldn't have been satisfied with seven canoe loads of rice. They would have wanted eight.

While sacking up, they laughed because one of the greedy ones tipped over right in front of the landing. The rice would grow good there next time.

At the auction the bids were all pretty good, and they ended up selling their rice to that buyer from McGregor. The buyer knew he was getting quality rice at a low price. The buyer didn't know, in addition to the good rice, he bought half a muskrat house, wet blue jeans, and some rocks with zero nutritional value.

As the sacks were being weighed, the buyer was pulling up on the sack to decrease the weight. On the other side a skinny brown hand was pushing down just a little bit harder.

The people laughed as they watched this ancient tug of war. They were familiar with this yearly ritual.

Luke and Dolly looked forward to the next day of ricing. It should be a better one because now she knew what she was doing out on the lake. She is pretty and pretty good at ricing, thought Luke.

Yup, ricing was here again.

mahnomin

Tobacco swirled in the lake
as we offered our thanks.
The calm water welcomed us,
rice heads nodded in agreement.
Ricing again, megwetch Munido.
The cedar caressed the heads
ripe rice came along to join us
in many meals this winter.
The rice bearded up.
We saw the wind move across the lake
an eagle, a couple of coots
the sun smiled everywhere.
Relatives came together
talk of other lakes, other seasons
fingers stripping rice while
laughing, gossiping, remembering.
It's easy to feel a part of
the generations that have
riced here before.
It felt good to get on the lake
it felt better getting off
carrying a canoe load of food
and centuries of memories.

CULTURE CLASH

Luke Warmwater and his old lady Dolly were riding down a gravel road on the reservation. Luke and Dolly were on a ride because they had the gas.

It was ricing season, but the lakes were closed so they could rest. The wind was combing the tangles out of the rice. They were glad because they knew they could harvest the next day.

Down the road they saw someone shambling along.

"A way day," said Luke, pointing with his lower lip.

"Ayah," agreed Dolly. "That's your brother, the one they call Almost, isn't it?"

"Yah, I wonder what the hell he's doing around here," said Luke.

From the way he walked, Luke knew Almost had been on a drunk. There was nothing unusual about that. What was unusual was the bloody washrag he held against his head.

Almost got into the car and said, "Hey, brother, you got a smoke?"

As Luke handed him one, he began complaining and explaining. He was complaining about the cut on his head and explaining how it happened.

"This gash must need thirty-seven stitches. How about a ride to the hospital?" Almost said.

"No problem," said Luke. "Put your seatbelt on—we're now riding in an ambulance."

"That old girl broke her frying pan over my head. You know, one of those cast iron ones. I knew I shouldn't have gone home yet," Almost moaned. "Sure, I've been on a drunk, but she was laying for me when I got home. She used that frying pan for something besides fry bread."

"We went ricing yesterday," Luke said.

"That bonk on the noggin did nothing to improve my hangover. She was yelling about that skinny Red Laker I passed out next to. I got out of there before she really got mad," Almost continued.

"We got 150 pounds of rice at Dead Fish Lake yesterday," Luke said.

He began the ritual of Rushing Him to the Hospital. He felt good about driving so fast. He was on a genuine mission of mercy, and he could bend and even break the traffic laws.

Luke's old car was holding up pretty good on the high-speed run. "She'll need a quart of oil by the time we get there," he said.

The cops sitting at the edge of town eating donuts didn't know of Luke's mission of mercy. All they saw was a carload of Indians weaving through traffic.

Donuts and curses flew through the air as they began one of their own institutions called High-Speed Chase.

One cop was screaming on the radio about the chase. The other was trying to keep track of all the laws that were being broken.

"Hey, all right, we got an official police escort," said Luke when he saw the red lights in his mirrors.

By this time Luke's escort had grown to three city squads, and deputies were coming to join the chase.

The ambulance came sliding into the hospital parking lot and stopped by the emergency room. Dolly got Almost out of the car and helped him into the building.

Luke drove over to where you're supposed to park and began congratulating himself on the successful run to the hospital. His troubles began when the cops got to the parking lot. They were excited about the chase.

"What's wrong with you, driving like that?" yelled a cop as he came running up to Luke.

"I wanna see your license!" screamed the second cop as he tried to wrestle Luke to the ground.

"Good, he's gonna resist arrest," said the first cop as he drew out his nightstick.

"My brother, Almost, is—" Luke got out before a

nightstick glanced off the side of his head and shut him up.

Luke gave up trying to explain and just began to fight back. He was holding his own and even took one of the nightsticks away. He threw that thing up on the roof so they'd quit hitting him with it.

The balance of power shifted toward the law and order as more cops piled into the battle. Pretty soon Luke was sitting on the pavement, a subdued and handcuffed Indian. There never is an easy way to end these things, he thought.

The cops jerked Luke up on his tiptoes and marched him into the emergency room. Luke's head needed some doctor attention after all those nightsticks. They laid Luke down on the table next to Almost.

"Matching stitches," growled Luke to his brother.

"Anin da nah," said Almost and then shut up when he saw the cops and cuffs.

There was something ironic about the whole situation, but Luke couldn't figure it out as the doctor stitched the brothers up.

The cops took Luke to jail. On the ride, Luke saw the ripped uniforms and lumps on the cops. That would explain why they put the cuffs on so damned tight.

Luke was pushed into his usual cell block, and he checked himself for damages. It was good to get those cuffs off.

A cop came in and handed Luke his copy of the charges. In addition to traffic charges, there was one for theft of city property. They couldn't find the nightstick he threw away.

The cell block door clanged open, and Almost was pushed in.

"We gotta stop meeting like this," sighed Luke. "What they got you for?"

"Disorderly conduct and, of course, resisting arrest," said Almost.

"We'll go to court this afternoon," calculated Luke.

"When I got out of the hospital, the cops were still outside. They must have been mad yet because when I offered to drive your car home, they attacked," said Almost as he rubbed his cuff-damaged wrists.

So Almost went to jail, the car went with the tow truck, and Dolly went visiting relatives to raise bail money.

She got back to the jail as the brothers were being taken to court.

"Got you covered," she said as she flashed the bail money.

Luke grinned hard at her.

In court, the brothers Warmwater pleaded not guilty and demanded a jury trial. A new court date was set and the matter of bail came up.

Luke got up and addressed the judge.

"Your honor, I hate seeing you under these conditions. I've been here before, and as you may recall, I've always showed up on time for court.

"Ricing comes only once a year. The harvest is good this year and my old lady, Dolly, is finally learning how to make rice. I'm sure you know how important to the Indian people the rice crop is.

"The reason I'm telling you all this is because I'd like to request a release on my own recognizance."

"Request granted," the judge said as he galeved the case down the court calendar.

As long as he had the judge's ear, Luke got brave and said, "Oh, yeah, your honor, all that stuff is true for my brother too."

The judge cut them both loose. They walked out of there free ricing Indians. They used the bail money Dolly raised to rescue the car and to buy that quart of oil they needed.

They dropped Almost off at home. His old lady was kind of sorry about hitting him. When he promised to buy her a new frying pan, she forgave him. They began making preparations for ricing the next day.

Luke and Dolly continued their ride down the gravel road on the reservation. Down the road, they saw someone walking.

"A way day," said Luke, pointing with his lower lip.

"Don't you dare stop, Luke Warmwater!" said Dolly.

brown and white peek

What's it like living on the rez?
I'm always asked.
It's living near a lot of relatives
ready to help or gossip about your need for help.
The word reservation is a misnomer
reserved for who?
The white man owns 80 percent of my rez, Fonjalack.
Living there means finding something good
in something grim.
Glad for our chronic unemployment
when the white guys get lung cancer
from breathing asbestos at the mill.
70 percent unemployment on the rez
go down the road a few miles, it's 5 percent.
We have TV, that window to America
we see you, you don't see us.

I watch the news every night, whenever they show
Indians, it's always the same tired tub of walleye
maybe some kind of bingo doings.
Commodities are good for you, our nutritionist says.
Right, they let your stomach know your swallower
still works, eat them for the bulk, not the taste.
Rice Crispies now come in commods, in addition
to the Spanish lesson printed on every box and can.
Cereal de arroz tostado, anyone?
We live strong 'cause we know we're just one of
the generations of the people called Anishinaabe.
Our spirituality protects us from the excesses
of the manifest destiny dominant society.
What's it like living on the rez?
Come walk a mile in my moccasins
maybe we can pick up some commods.

GOOSE GOOSE

The cold spell had gone on for three weeks. Cars were breaking down. Dead batteries, broken door handles, and frozen gas lines added to the misery of the cold.

It had kept everyone inside. Only essential trips were made: groceries, medical appointments, court, and bingo.

The people of the reservation were warm, but the inside living was starting to wear on the nerves. A virus called cabin fever was sweeping through the community.

With the arrival of above-zero temperatures, the Sawyer Indians began leaving their homes. The drinkers went to the taverns to meet others of their own kind. The AA people went twelvestepping to their meetings.

Luke Warmwater didn't go to an AA meeting. He walked over to his friend's house. In the driveway, Louie Wise Owl was methodically kicking his car. It had bootprints and dents where Lou had connected. He was kicking like he was mad, not like a used-car buyer kicking tires.

"This coldhearted car. In July, if a kid walked by eating an ice cream cone, this pig would need a jump," complained Lou.

"I had one like that. When someone in the neighborhood opened the refrigerator, the gas line would freeze," answered Luke.

"Okay, okay, you win. You had a worse car than me. Like I always say, the first liar never has a chance."

"Get in and try it. I got the battery charger hooked up."

"Hah, you better do it. I think the car knows it's me."

"Where are the keys?" asked Luke.

"Where else? Frozen in the driver's door."

"Did you try heating them with a match?"

"No, does that work?"

"Yup, it's an old Indian trick. A Finlander from Cromwell showed me that one," said Luke.

"That's when it became an old Indian trick, right?"

"Yup, up until then it was an old Finlander trick."

The motor fired after a while. Lou unhooked the cables while Luke kept the car running at a fast idle.

"Let's take this old pig for a ride. I gotta charge up the battery," said Lou. "It's got a dead cell."

"Okay, where do you want to go?"

"Let's go to Bob's Tavern, see who else is moving around."

"I thought you were barred for life—something about that last fight there."

"Gawain, I can drink there again. I'm making payments. I almost got that window paid off."

"You shouldn't have hit that guy so hard."

"Who thinks of that stuff in the middle of a fight?"

When they got to the tar road, they saw Rod Grease walking. He was headed for Bob's.

"Hey Rod, you got that five I loaned you?" asked Lou.

Rod got in the cat.

"If I had five dollars, I'd be home guarding it. I got enough for entrance fee though," said Rod, pointing with his lips at Bob's Tavern.

Luke, Lou, and Rod went in the tavern. They were going to warm up with a couple of cold ones.

"Cold enough for you?" asked the bartender.

He brought a round to the table for the three thawing Sawyer Indians. Lou paid for the beer with a twenty dollar bill.

"Keep the change," said Lou. He was making another payment on the window.

The weather stripping screeched on the front door.

Their three heads turned as if jerked by a single string. Another cabin fever sufferer was coming in. It was Dunkin Black Kettle.

"Look who blew in from Perch Lake. Did you freeze out?" asked Luke.

"Gawain, I've survived over forty of these winters. I just wanted to see people again," said Dunkin.

Lou signaled for another round. Another Sawyer Indian was warming up with a cold one.

"Cold enough for you?" asked the bartender.

"Yah, it seems like every year I put my long johns on earlier and take them off later," answered Dunkin.

"Uh huh, and when you get to be an old man, you don't even take them off in the summertime," said Luke.

The skins at the table laughed. They had seen old men like that. They laughed as they pictured themselves in long johns in July.

"That reminds me of my brother Jeff," said Luke.

The way Luke said it made it a story, almost like the title of a book. He had the floor.

"It was when he was a little kid, two, three, years old. He was too young to know any better. Nobody owned up to it, but someone taught Jeff the goose, goose game.

"He knew if you poked someone between the cheeks with a finger and said "Goose, goose," they would jump and everyone would laugh. It worked every time.

"One afternoon, a white social worker came to the house. She was doing some kind of a survey. We'd seen her before. One of those white-glove kind of social workers. Her name was Miss Something or Other.

"We were all standing around the yard when she drove up. She got out of her car and walked toward the house. Miss Something or Other was having a hard time walking. Her high heels and our gravel. She dropped her clipboard. She bent over to pick it up. Jeff saw her. He went running toward her. His finger was sticking out. I ran to catch him, so did my sister Doris. I don't think I ran as fast as I could have. I wanted to see what would happen. Doris was running pretty slow too.

"Jeff connected. 'Goose, goose,' he said. She squealed and jumped out of one shoe.

"His brown finger left a mark that could be hidden only by sitting on it. She dropped her clipboard again.

"She hid the mark by sitting on it in her car. She never did come back for the clipboard. Doris and I were behind the house laughing. I could hear my ma and dad laughing in the kitchen.

"Goose, goose," said Luke, ending his story.

The Indians around the table laughed. The bartender laughed. Hell, even the owner of the tavern laughed.

"Goose, goose," said Dunkin. Everyone chuckled again.

In the tavern that night, many stories were told. The one most people talked about was "Goose, Goose." Some of the Indians were pretending they were Jeff, especially at the pool table.

During the course of the evening, one car was sold, twenty-seven scary pool games were played, and the jukebox never shut up.

Two macho guys went outside to fight. When no one came out to break them up, they quit.

The lights came on in the tavern. The bartender announced closing time. He unplugged the jukebox and announced it again. Twelve-packs were lined up on the bar, ready for their brown paper jackets.

Rod Grease had been snagged by a new woman. He bragged, "We're going to take a shower together, goose, goose."

Louie Wise Owl went home with his ex-ex-girlfriend. She was the one he broke up with before his current ex-girlfriend. It looked like they were both frantically looking for whatever brought them together in the first place.

"Hey Luke, take my car home, will you?" said Lou.

"Yah, my wife will bring it over in the morning," said Luke.

The tavern parking lot was empty except for one other car. That car owner was miles away, lying to a woman, not his wife, about his wife.

Luke looked around for Dunkin because he had promised him a ride. He went out to start the car, but it wouldn't start. When Luke opened the hood, he saw the battery was missing. Someone had stolen the bad battery.

Luke and Dunkin walked home through the squeaky snow. When they split up at the corner, one of them said, "Goose, goose."

walking through

The sun woke us up.
Urn pa o wasta we and I walked.
The logging road brought
memories, sunshine, and plans
we found a way through the swamps
the mud clung to us as we admired
the trees, the tracks, the quiet.
We saw and felt an old sugar bush
the wigwam frame is in a good location
the oneness we felt with what the Creator
made, brought us closer together
our marriage is building on solid ground
we found an eagle feather
we gathered cedar, sprinkled tobacco,
picked a rock from Perch Lake
we watched the sun go to sleep
as we continued our journey through
life, together.

WEWIIBITAAN

The hard oak bench was slowly numbing Hary's ass. He was bored. Still, it was a nice break from the routine of sitting in the county jail, juvenile section.

Sitting right behind the fostered, group-homed Indian was a huge, square-build deputy sheriff. He was there to make sure Hary had his day in court. The deputy was also there to make sure that Hary didn't run from his day in court. They sat, waiting for the judge to make his dramatic, black-robed entrance.

The court stenographer waited with her fingers poised over her skinny typewriter, ready to record the proceedings.

The court clerk sat next to the judge's chair. She shuffled her papers. The clerk was proud of her ability to make order out of chaos. Her schedule was being followed. She touched her beauty-shop hair as she studied the first case on the docket.

The clerk saw a good-looking, long-haired, wiry boy. He was wearing oversized jail coveralls. His black hair and brown skin made her suspect he was an Indian. Another one, she thought. The documents identified him as Hary Pitt, age seventeen, an escapee from a court-ordered group home placement. The boy was casually looking around the room.

Their eyes caught. The clerk was surprised to see such a defiant look. He was looking at her with eyes that said "Go ahead, do your worst."

She suddenly found some papers in front of her that needed shuffling. She thought she could feel his eyes boring into the top of her head as she looked down. She touched her hair again.

Hary smiled inside after winning the staring contest with the old white woman with stiff hair. Next he thought he'd try the stenographer.

Just as their eyes met, the judge swept into the room. The stenographer jumped to her feet, and so did the clerk. The deputy poked Hary to make sure he got up to show respect. Hary jumped to his feet so fast the deputy stepped back in surprise.

The judge surveyed the room and told everyone to sit down. The elderly bailiff had just struggled to his feet when it was time to sit down. The bailiff eased back down into his chair. He looked at the judge.

The judge asked the clerk if they were ready to proceed. The clerk, with some disapproval in her voice, said the attorney for the first case wasn't there.

Just then the defense attorney came into the courtroom. He was walking fast and his eyes were darting around the room. The attorney was carrying about a foot of files. He was pawing through them as he walked to the front of the room.

Juris McBrief was the attorney. He worked for Indian Legal Assistance. He asked Hary, the only Indian in the courtroom, for his name. Hary told him. Juris went through the files again. He then asked Hary if he was sure his name was Hary Pitt. Hary told him it was.

When Juris couldn't find the right file, he asked the judge for a short recess. The judge looked pained as he granted it and went on to the next case. Juris looked through the files while Hary watched the next case go through the wheels of justice. It was a drunk-driving charge.

The contrite driver pled guilty. The driver was given a thirty-day jail sentence. It was to be suspended if the drunk completed an alcohol treatment program. Hary thought he'd take a treatment program if they offered him a suspended sentence.

Juris finally found Hary's file. He read it as they waited for their turn in front of the judge. The file said Hary had been in a series of foster homes for the last three years. When Hary continued to run away to return to the rez, he was placed in a strict, structured group home.

Hary had liked the group home. There were a lot of rules, but Hary was streetwise. He knew how to get along wherever he was.

One group home rule required proper, timely notice before home visits. Hary had wanted to get out to visit his uncle who was home from the marines. Hary asked for a home visit. Since he had been guilty of numerous infractions of the rules, the request was denied. They were minor infractions but were infractions nonetheless. Hary was also in trouble in summer school.

When his visit was denied, Hary had made a break for it. He hitchhiked to the rez after school. He knew from his past escapes how long he had before the cops started looking.

Hary had been on the run for three days before he got scarfed up by the cops. The bulls grabbed Hary as he was walking down the road. He was hitchhiking back to the group home, but the cops didn't believe him. He had gone to the county jail. He had spent three days there before court.

Juris McBrief conferred with his client before the hearing. Even as they talked, Juris knew he was supposed to be in another court, with another client.

Hary told his attorney he hadn't wanted to stay away from the group home. He just wanted to run for a while. Hary wanted to be free on the rez. Juris nodded and thought of what he'd tell the next judge at the next courthouse.

"I was on my way back when they arrested me," said Hary.

"That's what they all say," said Juris.

Juris McBrief was a second-generation lawyer. His mother had steered him to and through law school. She wanted him to join her small family law firm after doing pro bono work. Juris was to gain experience from nonpaying clients rather than real ones.

When other Americans were splashing through the rice paddies in Vietnam, Juris was living at home and struggling through contract law. Because of his generational guilt, Juris went to help the Indians. His parents had imbued him with a sense of duty and a feeling of compassion for his fellow man.

Juris was dressed in a gray "trust me" suit (he had read the book on how to dress for success). His small salary allowed him to buy only off-the-rack clothing. He looked like a big kid. Juris wore his dirty blond hair kind of long. His pierced ear held a turquoise chip. His shaggy mustache went from his nose to just south of his mouth. Small pieces of Maalox tablets were clinging to his facial hair.

He had started to depend on Maalox when he lost his idealism defending Indians. He was fast approaching burn-out and was ready to fly home to mom.

"I'll ask the judge if he will allow you to return to the group home. The files say you're almost eighteen."

Hary laughed to himself. The files were wrong. He had turned eighteen while he was on the run. His date of birth was wrong in the files. Hary hadn't told anyone. It was his secret from the system.

Hary told his attorney that escape from a group home was a status offense. Since he no longer had status as a juvenile, he should be released. The defense attorney agreed.

Juris argued for his client. The judge didn't believe him. He wanted to see a birth certificate. It wasn't in the file. The judge decided Hary should wait in jail while a copy of the birth certificate was found. The stiff-haired clerk was dispatched to search for it. Juris rushed off, late again.

The deputy poked Hary for his elevator ride and walk back to jail. They stood and waited for the elevator.

While looking around the deputy, Hary could see the long, wide, polished hallway. He could see a red emergency exit sign at the end of the hall.

The elevator arrived, and Hary was pushed in. Just as the doors were almost closed, Hary made his move. He pushed the deputy and slipped through the crack of the closing doors. The surprised deputy was in for a solitary ride to the basement. Hary could hear him swearing.

Hary was free. He looked one way down the hall. It was empty. He looked the other way and was shocked to see a probation officer just coming out of an office. The probation officer dropped the files he was carrying and ran toward Hary.

Hary took off. He slammed through the emergency exit and hit the steps, taking them four at a time. The PO was just behind him. His adrenaline and fear were adding speed to his legs. He got outside and looked for the nearest woods.

Hary dashed through traffic. The PO was on the other side, waiting for a safe opening. Hary saw him there as he turned and looked. He threw the guy a Sawyer wave as he hit the brush and disappeared from view.

Hary's heartbeat slowed as he got deeper into the woods. He was in his own world now. Woods were familiar to him. He thought of where to go. If he headed directly to the rez, the cops would be waiting. He thought he'd circle them and get back that way.

In the meantime, Hary could hear the PO running through the woods. Should I outrun him or hide? thought Hary. He decided to do both. Hary hid in the brush until the PO ran by. Hary quietly followed him. The PO stopped running and bent over, his hands on his knees. He was breathing hard and his face was red. Hary went running by, full blast. The PO made a desperate clutching motion. Hary was ten feet down the trail when the PO's arms came together.

The PO tried running after Hary. He tripped on a piece of brush and went down hard. His pants were ruined. Hary ran on.

The bony Indian knew the squad cars would be arriving pretty soon. He wondered if that one deputy with the dog, Bobo, would be in on the chase. He continued deeper into the woods. Just for the hell of it, Hary would zig and zag as he ran. He felt like he could run all day.

The deputy and Bobo, the bulky German shepherd, found the PO lying on the trail. His leg and pride were hurt.

"That little bastard can really run," warned the PO.

"Don't worry, Bobo can catch him," said the deputy as he unsnapped the leash. The deputy radioed for assistance as the dog ran down the trail after Hary.

Bobo caught up with Hary after a fifteen-minute run. Hary splashed across Otter Creek. So did the dog. Bobo was barking as Hary turned to face him. The big German shepherd looked confused when he saw the Indian standing there. They stared at each other for a long time. Just for the hell of it, Hary yelled, "Sit!"

The dog looked around, walked in a small circle, and sat down. Bobo looked at Hary, waiting for the next command. Hary said, "Stay!"

The dog lay down. Hary strolled off with a confident air. Bobo watched him leave. The dog was wagging his tail.

Hary came to the edge of the woods. He would have to cross the state highway. Before he went out in the open, he lay down and looked it over. It was a good thing he did because a highway patrol car was coming down the highway. The squad car parked near Hary.

The cop faced the other way. Hary watched him for about five minutes. The cop looked bored. He got out of his car and walked around to the trunk. The cop dug out his thermos. He dropped the cap to the thermos as he was pouring coffee. It rolled under the car. Hary watched from the brush. When the cop knelt down to get the cap from under the car, Hary made his move. He dashed across the road.

Hary dove into the brush on the other side and turned to see if the cop noticed anything. The cop was still busy retrieving the cap from his thermos. Another highway patrol car pulled up. The cops angled their cars across the road and turned on the red lights. The first cop poured the second cop a cup of coffee. Jeez, I never had a roadblock before, thought Hary.

He turned and went into the woods. As he loped along, Hary heard the helicopter before he saw it. It was a highway patrol helicopter. Hary could read that on the floats. He ducked into a small balsam tree when the helicopter came close. He covered his sweaty face with his sleeves. Jeez, I never been chased by a helicopter before, Hary thought.

The helicopter moved away from Hary in its rectangular search pattern. Hary followed it for a hike because he was kind of lost. Hary took a reading on the sun and wasn't lost anymore.

Hary sprinted across a couple more roads and moved toward the rez. He came through the woods behind his uncle's house. Hary watched the house for a while. He was lying among the light green ferns. It was cool under the ferns. Hary could see without being seen.

The sound of a car caught his ear. It was a cop coming down the driveway to talk to Hary's uncle, Luke Warmwater.

Luke came out of his house and met the deputy in the driveway. Hary could see his uncle shaking his head no to the questions. The cop left in his squad car. Luke went back in the house.

There must have been some kind of radio message because the cop punched the accelerator when he was halfway out of the driveway. The rear wheels sprayed gravel as the car fishtailed for traction. The left turn signal came on just before the cop turned right. His red lights were flashing as he left. That looked like the same deputy I pushed in the elevator, thought Hary.

Hary walked up to the rear door with a bounce in his step. When he got up on the porch, he scratched on the doorframe. His uncle came to the door. He smiled when he saw his nephew.

"Bindigen, come in. We've been expecting you. The deputy says you're wanted for assault."

"I just pushed him, not even very hard. They had roadblocks, helicopters, and everything after me," Hary said.

"You should be glad they didn't use that dog Bobo on you," said Luke as he poured tea and put a bowl of fry bread on the table.

"They did. He caught me, but I told him to sit and he did."

"The dog listened to you?" asked Luke.

"Ayah, yes, I told him stay. and he did."

"Well, what are you going to do?" asked Luke.

"I don't know, maybe visit a little bit. I heard your brother was home from the marines."

"Ayah, he's over at your grandma's house."

"I guess I'll take a walk over there. Maybe I should run, you know, to stay in shape?"

A smart guy would stay on the trail to avoid a trip to jail," said Luke to his nephew. "Let me know if you need a ride later," he continued.

"I might need one back to jail after I'm done visiting."

Hary went on a trail to his grandma's house. He saw his uncle sitting in the backyard. Hary smiled and sat down next to him.

Hary's uncle told him about the Marine Corps. After listening for a while, Hary mentioned his great escape escapade. They talked the rest of the afternoon away. As the sun was touching the top of the trees, Hary decided to go back. He had talked with a lot of his relatives. The story of his escape and evasion was already on the moccasin telegraph. The telegraph worked faster since phones came to the rez.

Hary called his uncle Luke for a ride. Luke came over in his pickup. Hary wanted to play escapee right to the end. Instead of riding up front, Hary crawled under a piece of plywood in the bed of the truck. Luke laughed after Hary climbed in the truck.

Hary got out of the truck in front of the jail. He walked up and rang the bell. He was ready to face the music and take his medicine. He used up all his clichés as he stood there. Face it like a man, he told himself.

The same deputy he had pushed twelve hours earlier answered the bell. He grabbed Hary's left arm and pinned it behind his back. The deputy forced Hary to the floor and was swearing at him. Hary's face scraped on the concrete floor. He felt the sting but was more concerned with the big deputy kneeling on him. It was getting hard to breathe.

Another deputy came up and pulled the mad cop off Hary. He was taken to the booking room for his reentry into jail. Hary took a shower in the same cell block he was in before the escape. He crawled into his steel bunk. He was tired from his morning run and afternoon of laughter. He slept well.

After breakfast the next day, Hary went back to court. The clerk hadn't found his birth certificate. Juris McBrief showed up. He brought a certified copy of Hary's birth certificate. The judge accepted this and the escape charge was dismissed. The matter of the assault of the deputy in the elevator came up.

The judge saw the scrape on Hary's face. He asked if it happened while he was running in the woods.

"No, awain, the big cop standing behind me did it. When I turned myself in last night, the big guy threw me around," said Hary. The judge looked at the bony Indian and the big cop. The charge of assault was dismissed.

The clerk, sitting next to the judge, ignored Hary. He tried to catch her eye but couldn't.

Hary was surprised when the judge told him he could leave. Hary thought of the relatives he could stay with until he got a place of his own. Juris shook his hand and walked away rapidly. Juris was already late for his next Indian.

Hary thought he'd retrace his run through the woods on the way back to the rez. He wanted to relive his morning of glory.

On the way to jail to pick up his personal effects, Hary saw the deputy and Bobo. They were just getting out of their squad car. Just for the hell of it, Hary yelled, "Sit!"

The dog sat down.

one more number

"Bingo!" said my friend
sitting next to me.
I'm glad for her but I wish
even more it was me.

The tension mounts, I need one
more to make a small picture frame.
He called the one next to mine.

Am I using my lucky dauber?
Am I sitting in my lucky seat?
Oh well, I didn't want to win
right away, anyway.

My number comes up on the screen.
A new set of worries,
Did I make a mistake?
How many do I have to split with?

Bingo! I win, is it true if I win
once, the next win is easier now
that the pressure is off? No.

Should I play another extra game?
She bought the one I was going to buy.
If she wins. . .

Not too big of a crowd tonight
the odds tilt ever so slightly in my favor.

I need one more to blackout.
Will he call it?
If he does, I'll probably black out
from the shock.

The buzz of the crowd tells me I was
once again beat by a little old grandma.
Why doesn't she stay home?

I hate this game, I'm never coming back.
I wonder what time they
open tomorrow night?

BINGO BINGE

"I'm cashy. Shall we go to bingo?" Luke Warmwater said to his wife. "I sold that old junk car in the backyard for forty-five bucks."

"How much can we afford to spend?" Paneqwe asked.

"Oh, about forty-five dollars. Do you feel lucky?"

"My left hand has been itchy, but it's lied to me before."

"Let's try it. You never know."

Luke and Paneqwe drove the ten miles to the Fond du Lac Reservation bingo hall. Paneqwe liked to play at the local bingo hall. She seemed to win more often there. She also knew the bingo workers and their families. Luke liked it because the money stayed on the rez. As bingo players, they didn't qualify as hard core but were pretty damn close.

In its other life, the bingo hall was the school gym. The huge, gray, high-ceilinged building held two hundred bingo players, some of them hard core. Overhead, the silent scoreboard watched. Most of the floor space was taken up by ten rows of folding tables. Each table had room for twelve players. There was a red-vested worker for each row. In the back room were other games of chance: bingolette, bingo twenty-one, video bingo, and 20/20 bingo. The pull-tab boxes were lined up along the south wall of the cavernous building.

The pull-tabs cost a quarter to two bucks each. The brightly colored boxes grabbed the eye. The promise of hundreds of dollars in winnings grabbed the gambling spirit.

"I wish I had a dollar for every wish made here tonight," said Luke as they walked through the crowds.

"Right. Then we wouldn't have to sit here all night. We could just swing by, pick up our wish money, and leave," she said.

"If you stand in line for the bingo packages, I'll find us some lucky seats. Who do you want to sit by?"

"Let's sit by your sister Nita. She's always lucky; maybe some of it will splash over on us."

Luke resisted the pull of the pull-tabs. He walked right by them. His cousin Sarge hadn't. Sarge liked to wear beaded belt buckles. It was a shame no one saw them. His belly pushed them down so they were pointing at the floor. A person saw only the top rim of the pretty beaded buckles. Sarge was in the middle of a pull-tab frenzy, kind of like the feeding frenzy that sharks do sometimes. He ripped the tab open. He looked at it and threw the loser away. At the rate he was going, he could have opened fifty tabs a minute. His eyes never left the pile of garbage he was making.

"Doing any good?" Luke asked.

"Gawain, just donating tonight," said Sarge.

When Luke walked to the back of the hall, he saw a lot of his relatives playing the early-bird games. Some of them owed him money. I'll see if they get lucky tonight, he thought.

The hard-core players were already settled in their lucky seats. They had been outside in the parking lot, waiting for the bingo hall to open. The hard-core had their lucky charms spread out on the tables. Luke saw four-leaf clovers of various sizes. He saw lucky coins. There were a couple of waboose feet. He even saw a plastic Jesus from someone's dashboard.

Luke sat down by Nita. She personally didn't believe in lucky charms. She just got up and walked around her chair between games. The chair trick seemed to work because her winning streaks usually lasted longer than one night. Luke was tempted to try circling his chair. He didn't because he laughed at his sister for doing that.

"How much are you going to win?" he asked Nita.

"I don't know. What does it mean when your left foot is itchy?"

"Either you're going to win a lot of money, or it's time to change your socks," Luke teased.

"Since I change my socks every day, I'd better line up a guard to escort me home. It's your fault I'm here tonight, you know."

"Why me?"

"I heard you won the coverall for a thousand."

"Yah, easy come, easier go. I don't have a dime of that money left."

"Uh huh, that kind of money never seems to last."

"Will you laugh at me if I get up and circle my chair?" Luke asked.

"You bet," she said.

Paneqwe came to the table and sat down. She handed Luke his bingo package. She had bought two ten-dollar boards. She felt lucky but not lucky enough to buy the thirty-dollar boards. She also had a couple of the lucky seven boards.

"Did you get any pull-tabs?" Luke asked.

"Yah, I spent five dollars on skid row, the quarter tabs."

"Did you win?"

"Gawain," she white-lied.

When Luke looked away, she pulled a winning pull-tab from her purse. She was rat-holing. She liked to surprise him with her wins. When Luke looked back, she was holding the winner at eye level.

Luke smiled and turned it over to see how much she had won.

"Fifty bucks," she told him.

"That's good. Free bingo tonight," said Luke.

While Paneqwe played the early-bird games, Luke went to the bingolette tables in the back room. He helloed his relatives as he walked by.

Bingolette was a quick, simple game. A player put his bet down on any of the seventy-five spaces. The worker called the first five numbers out of the machine. If the player's number was called, he won twelve dollars plus his wager. It looked easy to win. It wasn't. The rez was not in the bingo business to give money away.

Luke watched the game for a while. He was trying to see if any of the numbers came out more often than the others. Sarge had left the pull-tabs and was now gambling on bingolette.

"Did you win at the pull-tabs?"

"After forty-five minutes, I was thirteen bucks behind," said Sarge.

"Looks like you're doing okay here," said Luke, pointing to the pile of green chips in front of Sarge.

"I'm making up for the money I wasted on those damn pull-tabs."

"Where do you get the numbers to bet on?"

"I pull them right straight out of my ass," laughed Sarge.

When Luke thought he detected a pattern, he bet. When he cashed in his chips, he was fifty-five bucks ahead. Free bingo.

He wondered how long he could go without telling his wife. He liked to surprise her with his wins.

Luke went back to join his wife and sister. It was time for the regular games to begin. There were no winners at their table during the early-bird games.

The caller welcomed the players to the bingo hall. He read the rules of the house. The caller repeated the rule about winning on the last number.

"We don't pay sleepers," he warned.

The first game was regular bingo. Someone they didn't know won that game. That was the pattern that developed over the next twelve games, someone else always won. In the hard-core player's language, no one had an "out," no one was "on." Luke got bored with losing. Paneqwe played his board while he went to gamble on the pull-tabs.

He was feeling expansive so he bought the expensive pull-tabs. He bought twenty dollars' worth. No winners in that bunch, so he bought twenty dollars' more. No winners. He got another ten dollars' worth of the pull-tabs for his wife to open. He was spreading the blame around for wasting so much money on pull-tabs. Paneqwe opened the pull-tabs between numbers called during the bingo game. No winners.

They were now on the last game before intermission. It was the large picture frame game. This one paid five hundred bucks to the winner.

The players at their table each put up a quarter for a side bet. The first one to get a hard-way bingo won the side bet. It added a little interest to the game.

"Remember, a hard way means no free or four corners," Luke said.

"Look at her over there. She's with a different guy again," Nita said, indicating one of their cousins.

"She must have spent that guy she was with last week," said Paneqwe. "I wonder what her old man will say when he gets out of jail?"

"It was probably his idea," said Luke, adding to the gossip.

"I hope she wins. She owes me money," said Nita.

The picture frame game was progressing nicely. Luke was using his lucky red dauber. When he daubed O-69, the dauber went rogue on him. It was giving out too much dauber juice. Paneqwe dug out a backup lucky dauber for him.

Nita won the side bet and was closest to winning the real game. She needed four numbers while everyone else at the table needed seven or eight. The caller called two of her numbers. She was starting to spend the five hundred bucks she would win. She only needed numbers fifty-seven and forty-eight.

"Under the G-57," the caller's voice boomed from the wall mounted speakers.

"I've got an out," she calmly said. She didn't remember if she had walked around her chair before the game started. Just to make sure, she got up and did it again. Luke chuckled.

"Under the B-13," said the caller.

"Under the I-29."

"Under the O-74," continued the caller. Each new number called brought a groan from the players. It sounded like there were quite a few that were close to winning. Nita needed the forty-eight.

Just to tease the players, the caller put the ball in front of the TV monitor, showing just the letter on the ball. All eyes were on the TV. The players at their table were wishing real hard for Nita.

"Under the G." There was a long pause before the caller rotated the ball so the number could be seen. It was forty-eight. Nita had a winning board. She threw her arm up so quickly, her elbow popped. It sounded like a rifle shot. She spent the five hundred bucks three more times before he called the number.

"Forty-eight."

"Bingo!" yelled Nita. She said it so loud that two little grandmothers jumped in the next row. They turned and looked at her with hard, flinty eyes. One reason was because she won and the other was because she scared them with her yell. Nita ignored them.

The red-vested worker came over and verified her winning board. Nita won the game by herself, no splitting.

"Nita, quick, loan me five hundred bucks?" Luke said when he saw some of their relatives working their way over to the winner. Nita was laughing real loud, a winner's laugh.

"Sure," she said when she saw the relatives coming.

"I don't really need it. Just tell those people coming that you owed it to me. I'll tell them no for you," said Luke.

"Good idea," Nita said. "I don't want to loan out any money tonight. Maybe I'll feel different tomorrow."

When the red-vested worker came over to pay off Nita, she handed the money to Luke. He put it in his pocket. Nita told the relatives she owed the money to Luke.

Luke just said, "No."

The almost-borrowers walked away grumbling. When the last of them left, Luke slipped the money back to Nita under the table. She gave out another winner's laugh at their under-the-table delivery. It was time for intermission.

During the intermission, the players got up to stretch and move around. Some went to the back room for bingo-lette and the video machines. A lot of the players went up to the pull-tab boxes. They were lined up three deep, thrusting their money at the workers.

Luke and Paneqwe went over to gossip with his cousin

Bage. She was a proud Chippewa woman. Her deep black hair captured the overhead lights.

"Was that you hollering bingo back there?" she asked Luke.

"Gawain, that was Nita. She hit on the picture frame."

"She's always lucky," said Bage.

On the table in front of Bage were her lucky charms. She had her kids' pictures, a small stuffed animal, and a large horseshoe.

"I came by your house and borrowed one of the shoes from the set you have in the backyard. No one was home. I'll bring it back tomorrow," said Bage.

"Is it bringing you any luck?" Paneqwe asked.

"Not yet, but it was good for a few laughs when I pulled it out of my purse and slapped it on the table," Bage laughed. She picked it up and clunked it back down on the table.

"Trying to shake a little luck out of it," Bage continued.

"If you win, you can keep the horseshoe," said Luke.

"If I win, I'll buy you a new set of horseshoes," she promised.

"Well, good luck then. We're going to crash through the crowd to get to the pull-tabs," said Luke.

Luke looked at the pull-tab crowd. It looked dangerous. Too many elbows flying around. Too many heavy women throwing their weight around. They watched the crowd for a while. Paneqwe couldn't hold out anymore. She confessed, "I opened two fifty-dollar pull-tabs earlier."

"I won fifty-five at the bingolette table," Luke confessed.

"I know," she said, remembering his swagger on the way back to the table.

"Do you want to go spend some of the bingo hall's money on bingolette?" he asked.

"I thought you'd never ask."

"I was waiting for you to bring it up."

"What color chips are lucky back there tonight?" she asked.

"I won it all using the pink chips," he bragged.

"Let's go see if they're still giving money away."

The bingolette balls were not kind to the Warmwaters. After losing steadily, they decided enough was enough and quit. They went back to the hall to wait for the start of the second half. The lucky seven game was played during this part of the evening.

The first nineteen numbers out of the machine were called. The players marked their boards with numbers between one and seventy-five before the game. If their seven numbers were called, they would win the big money. It was worth $11,750 tonight.

When no one won, they played the game for the consolation, a couple of hundred dollars. The game usually ended after about thirty numbers were called.

Paneqwe used birthdates for her lucky seven. She sometimes used ages. Luke used highway numbers. Everyone had a system for picking lucky seven numbers. It was possible to win this game: Luke's cousin once won more than twenty-two thousand dollars. When you're worried about the cost of toilet paper, twenty-two grand is a lot of money, she told him.

Luke's highway numbers were hitting. By the eleventh call he had four out of the seven. Now if they would only call six, thirteen, and twenty-six.

"I've got a chance at the big money," he whispered to his wife.

"Don't get happy, you know what always happens," she counseled.

"Now I just need thirteen and twenty-six," Luke said as he daubed the six.

"Under the B-12," said the caller.

"Right next door, call his older brother," begged Luke.

"Under the B-H," said the caller.

"Not that older brother," begged Luke.

"Under the I," the caller paused, "26."

Okay, just one more number, Luke prayed to the bingo gods.

The caller went through twelve numbers without calling another B. Finally someone on the other side of the hall won the game.

Luke crumpled up his boards and tried a hook shot on the trash basket. He missed that too.

The concession stand announced that prices were cut in half for cooked sandwiches. Sarge, a good knife-and-fork man, jumped up and headed for the window where sandwiches were sold. He loaded up on the polish sausages. Sarge had been waiting all evening for that particular announcement.

The bingo gods must have been out to lunch. The Warm-waters didn't win one game the rest of the evening. They tried a few more pull-tabs on the way out of the building. Nothing, just making the garbageman happy. No winners.

Luke checked his pockets once they got outside. He had forty-six dollars.

"Do you want to come back tomorrow night?" Paneqwe asked.

"We had fun, didn't we?"

"Yes, we gambled and gossiped."

"If he had called B-13, we'd really be cashy."

"We're a dollar ahead, still making money at the bingo hall."

"Shall we come back?"

"I don't know. Flip a coin."

barbed thoughts

I am Anishinaabe,
in the spring we spear fish
rez government wishes we wouldn't
it makes some white people mad.
That's par for the course
they've been mad at us
since they got here,
rednecks try to stop us
with threats, gunfire, and bombs.
The state attempts a buyout
thinking cash can do anything.
We're valuable to the media
we fill their columns and empty air
good people witness for us.
We thank Munido for fish, for life,
as we praise our grandfathers
and their generational wisdom.
Spearing is more than a treaty
right—it's an eating right.
We do what has been done since
there have been Anishinaabe.
I am one of them.
I spear fish.

JABBING AND JABBERING

"They said we'd get arrested if we go spearing off the rez," said Tuna Charlie.

"Who is going to arrest us for using our treaty rights?" asked Luke.

"Either the rez game wardens or those from the state," answered Sonny Sky.

The three Shinnobs were sitting in Luke Warmwater's backyard, carving knockers for next fall's wild rice harvest. It was a good five months before ricing, but they wanted to be ready. Mostly, they wanted to be outside, enjoying the spring weather on the Fond du Lac Reservation in northern Minnesota.

"Tribal government is supposed to protect our treaty," said Tuna.

"Yah, they're supposed to, but the state is offering them two million dollars if we don't use our treaty rights," said Luke.

"What a power trip. Just think, being able to decide where to spend two million," said Sonny as he stood up. "I'd bet a million bucks none of that two million will reach the people." No one wanted to take his bet.

He folded up his knife as the curls of cedar fell from his lap. Sonny looked down the length of the knockers, checking them for a warp. He made a couple of practice ricing strokes. The faint smell of cedar came from the pile of shavings at his feet.

"I'm ready for ricing now. Are we gonna go spearing tonight or not?" asked Sonny.

"Yah, let's go. I'm not afraid of jail," bragged Tuna.

"I don't think we have to sweat jail. We just have to worry about getting our stuff taken away. You know—spears, canoes, lights, batteries, and maybe the cars," said Luke. "After that, we'll have to show up for court."

"They can't catch us. We'll be using the treaty rights our elders gave us," said Sonny as he walked to his mostly primer-gray truck.

"Meet you at Tuna's house just before dark," yelled Luke.

Sonny agreed by giving out two brief beeps of his truck horn. He threw them a Sawyer wave as he left the driveway.

Tuna and Luke continued working on the knockers. Tuna used an ax to split the cedar log into quarters. Luke was roughing out the shape of the knockers with a hatchet. He was using an Atlanta Braves kind of a stroke. Luke sat back down and took out his knife to carve the cedar.

"How many of these are we making?" asked Luke.

"My ma needs a pair, and my cousin said he'd pay money for some."

"Two pair done, two more to go then."

The warm southerly breeze was shrinking the remaining snow. The crows were back; they could hear them cawing in the distance. It felt good to be sitting in the warm sun after the usual long, cold winter. Sugarbush was over so they were getting ready for ricing. There is always something to do to prepare for the next season, Tuna thought.

Ten miles east of the carvers, five other Shinnobs were sitting at a shiny conference table. It was the regular Tuesday morning meeting of the Reservation Business Committee. The chairman was sitting at the head of the table. He was sipping hot coffee.

"Let's get this over with. I have to be somewhere in an hour," said the chair, looking at his watch. The thick turquoise chunks on the watchband caught the morning sun.

"The state of Minnesota is going to give us two million dollars to forego our rights to hunt, fish, and gather in the ceded territory. They also said they'd give us all the walleye we want," reported the District One representative.

"That won't satisfy those dissidents from Sawyer. They're dead set against selling or leasing treaty rights. They say the rights belong to future generations," said District Two, as he spread butter on his sweet roll.

"What's wrong with those people? We're not living in the 1800s. We have to be pragmatic and try to get along with the state," said District Three, biting into his sweet roll.

"What are we going to do with the money?" asked the secretary-treasurer.

"We sure can't give out a per capita payment. We have to pay off that loan for the factory," said the chair. "We'll tell the people that we're using the money to build a war chest to protect treaty rights—call it research or something."

"I still don't understand why the factory went belly up," said District One.

"You were the one who wanted to hire your white friend from high school," accused District Two, reaching in front of District One to get the last sweet roll.

"I never would have guessed he would turn out to be a thief," muttered District One defensively.

"How long did he get away with it before we found out from the bank?" asked the chair.

"According to the auditors, about two and a half years," replied the secretary-treasurer, looking through his cigarette smoke.

"The manager we had before that wasn't too good either," said District One.

"At least he wasn't a thief—kind of stupid, but not a thief," said District Two. "He would overbid on some projects so we didn't get them and underbid on the ones we did get. That guy must have cost us a couple hundred thousand dollars."

"No sense living in the past. How do we get out of this current mess?" asked District Three.

"The only way I can see is to lease the treaty rights to the state. Besides, there are not many that use them anyway," claimed District One.

"Sure, you know why? The state has been arresting them for over sixty years. They call it poaching," said District Three.

"The Shinnobs from Wisconsin have been using their rights to hunt, fish, and gather off the reservation for a couple of years now," advised the chair. "It's the same treaty."

"Look what has happened. Did you see the protests on TV at the boat landings? I saw some angry white people swearing, throwing rocks at the spearers. I read one newspaper report about gunfire on the lakes," said District Two.

"Well, we sure don't want to get the white people mad, either at the boat landings or at the state capitol," said the secretary-treasurer. Five heads bobbed in agreement around the table.

"Notify the state we're willing to lease our rights for a year. We can even give a little per capita payment just before the next election. But first, we have to get the bank off our back," said the chair. "We can lease the treaty year after year."

"Okay, I'll call the bank, you have our attorney draw up the agreement. Maybe we can sign it before the dissidents find out," said the secretary-treasurer.

"Henry Buffalowind is already down in St. Paul. I think he has that tentative agreement with him. He's our lawyer; he'll keep it quiet," reported District Three.

"Don't let the media get a hold of this. You know how those bleeding heart liberals are," warned District Two.

"I hate those media bastards," growled the chair.

"Does anybody think we're taking on too much without letting the people know?" wondered District One.

Districts Two and Three glared at him. He took a drink of coffee to hide behind his cup.

"Nah, they elected us to make these decisions for them. They don't know half of the problems we face every day," said the chair, again looking at his watch. "Okay, it's decided then. We lease our rights to the state for one year. Let's see if we can find a make-work project to keep the renegades busy."

"We got that grant for fire protection. Let's hire the troublemakers to cut firebreaks around the houses," suggested District Three.

"Good idea. They'll be too tired from cutting wood to spend any time on the lakes," crowed District Two.

"Okay, meeting adjourned. I'm going fishing. I've got to pick up my new three-hundred-dollar graphite rod from the sports shop. The guy there said I could catch fish in heavy dew with that rod. I'll be gone for a couple of days," said the chair.

The five RBC members split up like they were accused of committing a great crime. Their work day was over at 9:30 AM.

Ten miles west of the meeting site, Luke and Tuna were done making knockers. They began to get ready for spearing. Luke had three spearheads; he just had to attach them to the spruce poles. His canoe was loaded on the car already. He had to rig up a light.

"I can use this spotlight. I'll take off the case and duct tape the bulb to my old motorcycle helmet," said Luke. "I've got enough wire to reach the battery."

"Okay, I'll fix the spears while you do that," said Tuna. He carved the spruce poles so they would fit the steel spearheads. Tuna sharpened the spears with a whetstone.

Later that afternoon they were ready to go. They drove to Tuna's house to meet Sonny and his partner Asibun.

Sonny's canoe was sticking out the back of his truck as he pulled up. The powwow tape could be heard before he shut the truck off. He had a thermos of coffee, some bologna sandwiches, and two extra car batteries.

"I've been charging these all day," said Sonny, pointing at his batteries. "We should have enough light."

"Where are we going?" asked Tuna. He gave Asibun a nod of hello.

"Take your pick. We have over three hundred lakes to choose from. I don't think we should go to a lake that has cabins," said Luke as he gave Sonny a spear to use.

"Let's just make this a short trip—see how the fish are running," said Sonny.

"Who all is going?" asked Asibun.

"Just us so far. I bet a lot of others will try it once they hear about us," Sonny said.

"Where are the game wardens?" Tuna asked.

"According to my police-band monitor, they are on routine patrol looking for deer shiners," answered Asibun.

"Let's go to Hook Lake," suggested Tuna.

"Where's that? I never heard of Hook Lake," said Asibun.

"A little farther down the line," laughed Sonny.

They all joined in the laughter as they saw Asibun had fallen for one of the oldest jokes on the rez. The Kingbird Singers could be heard as Sonny started up his truck. They convoyed off after picking a lake south of the rez in the ceded territory. The daylight was used up as they drove down the backroads. They doubled back a few times to make sure they weren't being followed. It sure is hard to sneak around with a canoe on top of the car, Luke thought.

The boat landing was deserted when they got there. The smell of thawing lake met them. It was ice covered except for a collar of open water fifty feet out from the shore. They hid the vehicles down an old logging road after dropping off the gear at the landing.

The Shinnobs offered tobacco to the Creator after getting in the canoes. Tuna was going to spear first while Luke paddled. Sonny was spearing while Asibun was acting as the motor. The canoes separated, Luke going one way around the lake, Asibun going the other. The paddlers stayed close to the shallows, where the walleye nests were located. They could see the male walleyes circling the nests, trying to fertilize the eggs. The battery-powered lights lit up the lake bottom. Some of the light reflected off the surface and bounced into the trees. They could see birds sleeping on some of the branches.

Sonny tensed when he saw something reflecting his light. He moved his spear over to jab at it. Asibun moved the canoe over closer to where the light was pointing.

"It's just a Budweiser walleye," said Sonny. "Keep paddling."

"Sure are a lot of beer cans down there," said Asibun.

Tuna was getting good at picking out the fish eyes from the beer cans that were cluttering the lake bottom. He usually speared the fish right behind the head. Tuna would then carefully bring the fish up and drop them down into the canoe. The splash of the fish when they came to the surface was the only noise they heard on the lake. They could hear the loons singing, but that didn't count as noise.

The canoes came together on the other side of the lake from the landing. The Shinnobs changed places in the canoe and the motor became the spearer. The Shinnobs decided to call it a night when they got back to the landing.

At the landing they counted their catch. Sonny's canoe held thirteen walleye and a largemouth bass. Luke's canoe held eleven walleye and three bass. One of the walleyes in Luke's canoe looked small compared to the others.

Sonny and Asibun teased Luke and Tuna about the small fish. They compared it to a minnow and called them baby killers.

"Anybody can spear those great big fish. It takes real skill to hit those small ones," explained Luke.

They laughed and loaded up the canoes and the rest of the gear. They drove straight home because the police band monitor told them the game wardens had gone home for the night. Both vehicles were full of spear-fishing stories. They ate the bologna sandwiches and drank coffee while driving home. The heaters were blowing hot to knock the chill off the spearers.

The four Shinnobs cleaned fish in Luke's backyard. It took less than a half hour to finish up. Luke took the pile of fish guts out to where the ravens would find them. The four agreed to deliver the night's catch to the Elderly Nutrition Program. The fish sticks on the menu were crossed off and walleye fillets were added instead. The elders of the community were going to eat fresh fish because of the spearers.

During the next two weeks, the spearers had several confrontations with the RBC and the game wardens. Shinnobs from all over the rez were going spearing. Threats and promises didn't stop them. Neither did the offer of free walleye from the state. The Reservation Business Committee realized they couldn't stop the people from getting fresh fish. They quit trying and called off the game wardens. The RBC got special permission from the state to allow Shinnobs to keep spearing.

There was no way to stop the treaty lease, however. The RBC began getting heat from the people for leasing their treaty. Other bands of the Lake Superior Chippewa were calling and faxing the RBC. Most of the messages were negative about the treaty lease. There was talk of a recall election. The RBC were called sellouts. In the midst of the troubles, Henry Buffalowind quit and went to work for another tribe on the other side of the state. The RBC was going to great lengths to avoid the media. Phone calls were not returned to anyone.

The RBC called a special meeting to decide what to do. It was held one evening in the chairman's garage.

"We got the bank off our back, but the people are mad as hell about the treaty," said the secretary-treasurer.

"Is there any way we can get out of it?" asked the chair.

"Nope. Buffalowind told me before he left that we're committed for a year," said District One.

"Notify the state we can't lease the treaty anymore. The state is already asking about next year's lease. We have to give them formal notice that we're not going to lease after this year," ordered the chair.

"I wonder how this will affect the next election?" wondered District One.

No one had an answer for him. The chair adjourned the meeting, and they went their separate ways. Three of them were thinking of updating their resumes.

In an effort to save face, the chair asked Luke and Tuna if he could go spearing with them some night. Luke agreed; Tuna didn't say anything.

Luke told the chair he would have to provide his own canoe, light, battery, spear, and partner. The chair decided on District Two as his partner. He hired Luke to make him some spearing equipment.

That night they all met at a landing north of the reservation. Earlier Luke had called some friends from the media. The newspaper and TV people were waiting at the landing when the Shinnobs arrived. The chair and District Two brushed off requests for an interview. They quickly launched their canoe onto the dark lake. They left so fast they forgot to offer tobacco. The chair was spearing and District Two was the motor. The TV cameras taped them as they were going out.

Luke and Tuna quietly followed fifty feet behind the first canoe. They didn't forget to offer tobacco. Luke was going after fish the first canoe missed. Tuna and Luke also wanted to keep an eye on their leaders.

Luke heard a short, sharp cry of surprise. He looked up, and his light showed the chair with his neck caught in a Y-shaped tree branch. The chair was pushed past the point of balance by the tree and District Two's paddling. He dropped his spear, which hit District Two a glancing blow. The chair jumped into the lake to keep the canoe from turning over. Luke and Tuna saw and heard the splash as their leader hit the icy water.

District Two, with thoughts of gunfire on the lakes, saw the chair leave the canoe. When the falling spear hit him, he thought he was shot. The inside of his mouth tasted like copper. He rolled out the side of the canoe into the cold water. The canoe turned over when he left it. The cold water made him give out a small yell. The frigid water started both of them shivering immediately.

Luke and Tuna paddled up to help them. The chair and District Two were standing in water that came to the tops of their shirt pockets. Luke helped them right their canoe and find their paddle and spear. The light and battery couldn't be found. Tuna could see their lunch floating away. They held the canoe steady while their leaders climbed back inside.

The chair and District Two decided to quit. When they headed toward the landing, Luke and Tuna glided off, still looking for fish. Luke could see the fish as their eyes reflected the light. He turned and looked back at the boat landing to check on their leaders.

The chair and District Two were surrounded by the media people. Their wet, cold clothes were steaming in the hot TV lights.

Luke flipped another fish in the canoe. Tuna loafed along and let out a small chuckle. He could feel the canoe shaking as Luke laughed. The two Shinnobs continued looking for fish.

1854–1988

We told them not to sell, but boochigoo
they had to do it anyway.
The bottom line is the bottom line.
You sold our birthright, you paleface Indians.
Faces pale from kissing the white man's ass.
The bottom line is the bottom line.
The State flashes chump change,
indigent Indians are buffaloed.
Hunting, fishing, and gathering
now have a dollar value.
The bottom line is the bottom line.
Our elders told us the money
will soon be gone.
They were right, it's gone.
They're already looking down
the trail for the next chunk of treaty cash.
The bottom line is the bottom line.
Money talks, whispers, threatens,
and finally seduces.
The bottom line is the bottom line.
Anishinaabe have survived
missionaries and miners,
timber barons and trappers,
we'll survive the bureaucrats
and policy makers.
Bury the sellouts deep, their
grandchildren will want to
piss on their graves.
The bottom line is the bottom line.

STORIES AND STORIES

Luke Warmwater's kids were crabby. One of them was coloring on his younger brother with a magic marker, another was kicking the table to see if he could spill the milk using only his feet, and the youngest was just whining.

There was nothing good on TV. They had seen all the movies on the VCR. Luke stopped it all when he offered to tell them stories. He gathered his children around his chair.

He told his kids about the time everyone was crabby when he was a kid. There wasn't a dance or funeral close by. There were no rabbits to snare. Luke said, "Grandpa used to tell us stories. Grandpa told us about a guy from around here who used to like to walk. He was a pretty good walker. One time he walked in the direction the sun comes from. He walked until he came to the ocean and couldn't walk any more. He was a walker, not a swimmer, so he stopped.

"We went along with the walker as he went through the woods to the ocean on the East Coast. We learned about people that were friendly and those who were mean.

"We saw the lakes and rivers, we saw the valleys and mountains, we saw everything the walker saw as Grandpa told the story. After Grandpa told us that story, he got up and went outside to the toilet. When he came back, he continued to tell us about the walker. Grandpa said the walker was gone for three ricing seasons before he came walking back.

"The walker told stories to all the people around here. He never had time for a wife or family. A couple years after he came back from the ocean, he took off again. This time he went in the direction the sun goes down. He didn't come back from that walk. We like to think he made it to the other ocean anyway. 'Yup, he sure liked to walk,' Grandpa said as he closed the story. He then got up to holler at the dogs, who thought they smelled waboose or something.

"Grandpa sat back down and told us about the brave

warriors who used to live around here. He said when they used to go to war with the Sioux, the people would gather here from Portage, Nett Lake, and what is now called Wisconsin. They would travel night and day to go fight the Sioux. Grandpa told us about the guy who was captured after he was wounded. The Shinnob was tortured and then they cut off his feet. The Sioux tied him to a stake and were going to roast him with a fire.

"While standing on his cut-off feet, the warrior pulled the stake up out of the ground. He used that stake as a huge club and was chasing the Sioux around until a dozen arrows cut him down. 'That's the kind of warrior that used to live around here,' Grandpa said.

"We sat around his feet as Grandpa told us stories. He was dressed in dark green wool pants, thick wool socks, wide suspenders, a long john shirt, and mischievous eyes.

"While he was telling the story, he kept time by tapping a drum only he saw. His hand was shaped around an invisible drumstick as he kept time on the arm of his chair.

"Grandpa got up to put wood in the stove. A puff of good-smelling smoke came out and joined us in the room, listening.

"His calloused, thick-fingered hands told more than half of his stories. His hands, arms, shoulders, and eyes all added to the stories as he was telling them. He got up, got some green tea, and came back and sat down.

"Grandpa said, 'One time I was walking in the woods. I was over by—you know where the plum bushes are by Perch Lake? Well, I was right there. I don't remember where I was going that day. It was just getting to be spring, the leaves were just starting to come out. It wasn't really thick yet, you could see pretty far in the woods. The loons were back. I could hear them.'

"'I just came to that last turn in the trail there when, holy jeez, a big deer jumped up right in front of me. The deer stood broadside and looked at me. We must have stared at each other for twenty minutes before I made my move.'"

"Grandpa's hands and arms slowly raised a rifle. His hands and arms settled that rifle into a good firing position. His head dropped down to look over the sights at his supper. His trigger finger slowly pulled back on the trigger. 'Boom,' he said. We could see the recoil rock him back.

"Grandpa looked over the rifle with his eyebrows signifying surprise. The deer was still standing there, looking at him. He sighted in again, he slowly brought his trigger finger back, 'boom.' The recoil drove him farther back in his chair.

"Another look, another surprise, the deer was still standing there, looking at him. He tried a third time. He pulled that mighty deer slayer in tighter; he took his time sighting in. It was a long time before we saw his trigger finger creep back, ever so slowly.

"Some of us watched him; some of us watched where the deer was going to fall. Some of us watched both places, back and forth, 'boom.' The recoil this time drove him all the way back in his chair. It knocked him speechless. We all began to ask questions: 'How could you miss?' 'How far away was he?' 'Whose gun did you have?' 'My grandpa don't miss.' 'How could you miss?' 'Was that a magic deer?'

"He sat up, raised that mighty deer slayer up again, sighted in, and slowly began to draw back on the trigger. Before it went off this time, he looked at us with smiling eyes and said, 'I didn't have a gun.' We knew this was the last story of the night. We went to our beds happy because we had a grandpa who told us stories. Some of us were repeating 'I didn't have a gun' as we went to sleep."

Luke Warmwater looked around. His kids were either sleepy or asleep. He got up and carried them to bed.

time wounds all heels

We fought America's longest war
baby killers, dope smokers, walking time bombs
was how they remembered us.
We gave our youth and were ignored
shrapnel hurts, nightmares are ravaging
but the wound that hurts the most
is the indifference of those who stayed home.
It started with the Wall, then welcome home
parades twenty years after.
It's getting popular to be a Vietnam vet.
Ron Reagan praised us, amnesty for the
Canadian-Americans, Jimmy Carter said.
Platoon, *China Beach*, and *Tour of Duty*
are now around to tell our story.
It's getting popular to be a Vietnam vet.
Too popular for me, I'm thinking of quitting.
I liked it better when we were ignored.
Going back to Vietnam is too scary for
this graying grunt, someone might remember me.
America, where were you when we needed you?
Graveyards and veteran's hospitals
are filled with your debris.
I'm a veteran of America's longest war, maybe.

LOOKING WITH BEN

Rinnnnng! The telephone noise shattered the middle-of-the-night quiet.

Luke Warmwater woke up. He rolled out of bed and went to the living room to find the phone. He knew if he could find it, he could make it stop ringing.

Rinnnnng!

Since it's the middle of the night, it means bad news, Luke thought. He homed in on the noise in the dark living room. On the other end of the plastic and wire was Ben Looking Back.

As soon as Luke figured out who it was, he knew it wasn't bad news. A call from his first cousin always meant a good story.

"Boujou neej, did I wake you up?" asked Ben.

"No, I had to get up and answer the phone anyway," mumbled Luke.

"Can you pick me up at the airport tomorrow?"

"Sure, what time?"

"Flight 276, supposed to get in at 10:42 in the morning. Are you going to be busy?"

"I won't be busy, I'll be there."

"See you."

"Yah, see you in the AM."

Luke went back to the bedroom and got under the Pendleton blanket. Paneqwe rolled over and said, "Was that Ben? You always laugh like that when you talk to him."

"Yah, he wants me to pick him up at the airport tomorrow."

"Where was he this time?"

"He didn't say, but I think he was in Washington D and C again. Someone told me he took his big bingo win and went traveling."

"I suppose he was playing tourist again."

"Must have been. It's one of his favorite games next to hanging out at the tanning salon."

"He always shows up at the funniest places, doesn't he?"

"Yah, he does. Did I tell you about the time I ran into him way out in the woods? It was on the other side of Perch Lake. I was out there walking around, you know, looking at spring. I had just crossed that crick, and when I turned the corner in the trail, there he was. He was just sitting on a log, having a smoke. He must have been out in the woods looking at spring too."

Paneqwe fluffed her pillow as she talked with her husband in the dark bedroom. It was warm and quiet there.

"Remember that time we had to leave really early for the meeting in Minneapolis? Ben was over by the Catholic church corner. I wasn't even surprised to see him there. It was five in the morning, and he was just hanging out at the corner. When we got to the meeting, there he was again. He was just standing on the corner, telling stories with the city Indians. I wonder how he got down there so fast? He must have passed us when we stopped to eat in Pine City. He's got good hitchhiking medicine or something." Luke laughed as he remembered the day he met Ben twice.

"I wonder what he brought back from Washington?"

"I guess we'll find out in the morning."

The next morning, Luke sat in the Duluth airport waiting room. He had just watched Ben's plane land on the runway. The deplaning and departing passengers were coming off. They herded up and hurried off, anxious to rejoin their luggage. Luke scanned the herd. No Ben yet.

Ben Looking Back was one of the last to leave the plane. He was walking down that long skinny hall, laughing with the flight attendants. The pilots with their briefcases were walking behind, laughing at something Ben had said.

He separated himself from the flight crew and walked toward Luke. Their eyes caught and both gave an almost imperceptible nod. The nod said a lot. It meant "I recognize you as another Indian, another relative."

Ben was what they call a BFI, a big fuckin' Indian. Macaroni had sculpted that body. He was built like a dark

Frosty the Snowman. A red headband held his straight black hair under control. Ben's black marble eyes always looked like they were on the verge of a smile. His round face easily relaxed into a half grin.

Ben softly shook hands with his cousin. They went to the coffee shop to wait for the herd to leave. As they sipped hot coffee, Luke asked, "How was your airplane ride?"

"This one wasn't too bad, but the one going to Washington was kind of fun," Ben said.

"What happened?" said Luke, putting on his listening face.

"The plane made a turn away from the White House to land at National Airport," said Ben, flying his hand in a banking maneuver and then down toward the table. "The guy sitting next to me said there are Secret Service agents armed with missiles on the roof of the White House. They will shoot down any plane that gets too close," he continued.

"We dropped down pretty fast after we lined up with the runway. The plane hit the ground hard," said Ben, as he flew his hand towards the table. He slapped his hand down to show Luke how hard they landed.

"We hit the ground so hard, my oxygen mask popped out and fell in front of me. I had just been through the drill so I knew what to do. I slapped that sucker on. I was just getting the elastic around my head when the flight attendant poked me in the shoulder. Above the roar of the reversing engines, she said, "Take that off, we're at ground level."

"I shook my head no because I wanted to show her I was paying attention when they did the safety drill. The yellow rubber mask was collapsing against my face because the oxygen wasn't turned on. I finally took that sucker off so I could breathe," laughed Ben. "Yup, we hit the ground pretty hard."

"Oh yah, before I forget, I brought you a present from D and C."

Ben dug in his Levi's jacket pocket and handed Luke a dull, brownish-red piece of rock. One side was smooth and the other was rough. Luke accepted it and put it in his jacket pocket.

"The Smithsonian Institution has a collection of Indian remains. They have over eighteen thousand bodies there, all tribes. I read about it in that Indian newspaper from Hayward. Since they collect Indians, I decided to collect Smithsonians. That rock I gave you comes from that castle-looking building on the mall. If every Indian who goes to Washington brings back a little piece, we can build our own Smithsonian right here on the rez," said Ben.

Luke patted his pocket to let Ben know the first piece of the Smithsonian collection was safe. He took it out and looked at it real close, put it back, and signaled the waitress.

The waitress smiled at Ben as she brought the check. Ben tipped her handsomely. The two skins got up to go down to get Ben's duffle bag. She watched them walk away and said, "See you next time, Ben."

"I'll see you the time after next," he said.

Luke paid the ransom for his car and they left the parking lot. As they headed toward the reservation, Ben picked up where he left off.

"Washington sure is a funny place. The tourists would come up and ask if they could take my picture. Some of them sent their kids to stand next to me. Most of them sounded like Americans."

"After the first dozen, I started charging five dollars a pose. I made two hundred bucks in a little over an hour. I got tired of the dumb questions about Indians, though. Just for the hell of it, I changed tribes. With some of them, I was a Chippewa, with others, I was a Sioux. Sometimes I'd be a Comanche, and right at the end there, I was telling them I was half Chippewa, half Ojibway, and the rest was Anishinaabe. Some of the tourists were writing this stuff down as I talked. I had a good time with the tourists," Ben concluded.

"I'm gonna go with you next time. I like having my picture taken," said Luke.

"I had the most fun in one of those museums at the Smithsonian. I found the one that has Indian history. It was a big hall. They had a lot of dioramas and displays of Indian stuff. One of the diorama spaces was empty. They must have been changing the thing or something. Just for the hell of it, I made a sign out of a piece of cardboard. I wrote Contemporary Chippewa and propped it up," said Ben, as he showed Luke the size of the sign with his hands.

"I stepped over that velvet rope, turned around, and just stood there. Pretty soon, some tourists came by. They read the sign and looked up at me. I was standing there as still as I could. They looked at me a long time before they went on to the next display. I relaxed a little until I heard some more coming. I got some strange looks from them. One guy was looking back and forth, first at the sign, then at me," said Ben, showing Luke how the guy was looking back and forth.

"The next couple of groups walked by without even seeing me. The ones after that stopped and looked. A woman unsnapped her camera bag and snapped a picture of me. She was careful to get me and the sign together. After the flash went off, I broke my pose, stepped toward her, and said, "That'll be five dollars please." He showed Luke how he held out his hand to receive the money.

"She took her camera off her eye, looked around, spun, and took off. I thought she was going to get a guard so I stepped back over that velvet rope. I left the sign up, though. As I was walking away, I saw more tourists reading the sign and looking at the empty space," said Ben, showing Luke how the tourists were looking.

By this time, Luke was laughing so hard he had to pull the car over on the side of the road. After he settled down and wiped his eyes, he was ready to continue the ride home to the rez.

Luke dropped Ben off at his house. He then went home. He and Paneqwe were going shopping at the mall.

Paneqwe poured a couple of cups of coffee and sat at the kitchen table. Luke came in, sat down, and thanked her for the coffee. She put on her listening face.

Luke told her the Ben Looking Back stories of the trip to DC. She laughed hard and said, "I can just see him stepping over that velvet rope." She stood up, stepped over an imaginary rope, and struck up a contemporary Chippewa pose. She giggled her way out of the pose.

Luke tried it. He stood up and stepped over the rope. He stuck his hands in his jacket pocket, tilted his head back slightly, glazed his eyes, and stared off in the distance.

Luke held his pose until Paneqwe poked him in the ribs. They finished their coffee and went out to the car.

"Remember that time he was on a media kick?" she asked.

"Yah, every time I turned on the TV, there he was. He somehow got in the background of all those news stories. If they were showing a car-crash story, there he was, looking at the wreckage, maybe reconstructing the accident. I saw him at the reception they had for the governor. He was just standing there watching the doings. On that bike-a-thon story from Sawyer, he was there to see them off and then welcome them to the finish line. Ben was everywhere. He must have a media magnet in his pocket. He always seems to be in the wrong place at the right time."

"I used to be surprised about the way he turns up everywhere; not anymore," she said.

Luke and Paneqwe walked into the mall. As they turned the corner by the tanning salon, they saw Ben. Luke remembered that Ben liked to hang around at the artificial sun place. He didn't openly laugh at the frog-belly-white people that went in. He just sat outside, offering his brown skin as a standard. Almost like saying, this is what you're supposed to look like.

After the nod both gave, Ben said, "She's been in there too long," pointing with his lips at a lobster-red white woman.

"I bet she'll peel in big sheets," said Luke.

"Why do they do that? They hate Indians but try to look like them," said Paneqwe.

"I don't know; they always want something they can't have."

Just then, a local TV crew arrived. After asking, Ben found out they were there to do a story on tanning salons. Ben was in his glory. He was going to be on TV at a tanning salon.

Luke and Paneqwe slipped away to buy groceries. They shopped and went home. After supper, Luke turned on the TV to watch the evening news.

They saw Ben Looking Back looking back at them on the TV. His brown skin was a sharp contrast from the white people in the story.

Rinnnnng!

It was Ben on the phone asking for a ride to the airport.

"I'm going to San Diego. I got some of that bingo money left. I heard there is a nude beach by La Jolla, Black Beach, or Bart Beach, something like that. They must get good tans there," said Ben.

"San Diego?"

"Yup, the plane leaves at two in the afternoon."

"Okay," Luke laughed.

He was already looking forward to the California nude beach stories. Paneqwe smiled.

ogichidag

I was born in war, WW Two.
Listened as the old men told stories
of getting gassed in the trenches, WW One.
Saw my uncles come back from
Guadalcanal, North Africa,
and the Battle of the Bulge.
Memorized the war stories
my cousins told of Korea.
Felt the fear in their voices.
Finally it was my turn,
my brothers too.
Joined the marines in time
for the Cuban Missile Crisis.
Heard the crack of rifles
in the rice paddies south of Da Nang.
Watched my friends die there
then tasted the bitterness of
the only war America ever lost.
My son is now a warrior.
Will I listen to his war stories
or cry into his open grave?

REZ TO JEP TO REZ

The birch and popple leaves were yellow. The red of the maple had come and gone. It was warm in the afternoons.

Luke Warmwater and his wife for life, Paneqwe, were making rice in the backyard. Their part of the season's gift had been harvested and parched. She was dancing and he was fanning.

As they worked, they watched the occasional car going by the house. They talked about the people that went by. The cars they didn't recognize were automatically classified as tourists. A familiar car went by.

"That's your cousin, isn't it?" she said.

"Yup."

"How are you related to him?" she asked.

"Let's see now. . ." Luke paused in his fanning. He resumed fanning and said, "His dad and my grandma on my dad's side were brother and sister."

"Your cousin, huh?"

"Yup, my cousin."

Paneqwe enjoyed the *shish-shish* sound the rice made as she danced. Luke looked closely at his fanning basket. He was thinking how it could be made better next year. Luke liked the color of the translucent green rice. It made a rhythmic sound as it bounced in the basket. The empty hulls drifted with the wind.

A customized van pulled into the driveway. They didn't recognize it until the driver got out.

"Looks like Dave has got himself a California van."

"I wonder what he wants? He usually doesn't visit us."

"I guess we'll find out. Here he comes."

Dave walked over to where they were working. He said hello to both of them. Dave settled into a lawn chair and said, "Who'd you learn that from, making rice?"

"From everyone I ever watched," answered Luke.

"My grandmother used to make rice like that."

"Not many people do it this way anymore."

"It's so much easier to do it with machines."

"I think hand-finished rice tastes better," said Luke.

"It cooks easier too," added Paneqwe.

They were about done making rice for the day. She covered the pit she was using. Luke gathered up the baskets and rice. He carried the rice and baskets inside. The hand cleaning could be done as they watched TV. Luke invited Dave in for coffee.

They sat down in the living room and drank coffee. Dave talked about paddy rice.

"That paddy rice sucks. My wife cooked some for an hour and a half and it still wasn't tender."

"I've heard it called driveway rice," laughed Luke.

"Driveway rice?"

"Yah, when you get stuck in your driveway, you throw that stuff under the wheels for traction."

"That's about all it's good for," said Paneqwe.

Luke rewound the tape on the VCR as they talked.

"Want to watch *Jep* with us?" Luke asked.

"Sure, I like *Jeopardy!*" he said.

Watching *Jeopardy!* was a family tradish with the Warmwaters. They liked to match wits with the chimooks on the tube.

Luke was having a good day, snapping out the questions before the contestants. Dave was mentally keeping track of Luke's winnings. On Double and Final Jeopardy! Luke always yelled, "All of it."

When Final Jeopardy! was over, Luke was thirteen thousand dollars ahead of the players on the program. He always bet the entire amount because this was only TV.

"Do you always do that?" asked Dave.

"Make rice? Sure, every year," answered Luke.

"No, I mean play *Jeopardy!* like that."

"We usually watch it live unless we're doing something; then the VCR watches it for us."

"Do you always win like that?"

"Oh sure. For a compulsive reader, it's easy," bragged Luke.

Dave thanked them for the coffee and left. A plan was forming as he walked out to his van. Luke and Paneqwe continued cleaning their rice.

Dave came to the Warmwater house again the next day. He said he wanted to learn how to make rice. Luke let him do some fanning. When he spilled some on the ground, Luke suggested he should also learn how to clean rice. He sat him down where there wasn't a chance of spilling any more rice.

Once again, they went inside to drink coffee and watch *Jep* with the VCR. Luke was having an even better day, snapping out questions. Dave took out a small calculator and kept track of Luke's earnings. When Luke doubled his winnings on the Final Jeopardy! question, Dave proposed a deal.

"If I pay the costs out there and back, make all the arrangements, would you split half and half, you know, fifty-fifty?"

"Maybe," said Luke in a noncommittal monotone.

"Yesterday, I called Merv Griffin Enterprises. I got an appointment for you to take the test, a preliminary screening."

"Where is 'out there'?"

"Hollywood, we have to go to Hollywood. We can go in my van, take turns driving."

"I'll let you know tomorrow," said Luke.

After Dave left, Luke and Paneqwe talked about going to California. They were almost done with making rice so they had the time.

"Why not? It would make a nice break from the rice."

"I haven't been out there in quite a while," she said.

Luke called Dave and told him they were ready to leave for California. Dave came to their house. Luke threw their clothes and a cribbage board in the van. They left the rez.

The freeway was boring through Iowa and Nebraska. Luke and Paneqwe played cribbage in the back of the van. It was all long rolling hills, each crest about five miles from the last one. Luke kept expecting to see something different at each crest. He didn't; each crest looked the same as the last. The freeway looked the same all the way to the mountains.

The mountains were more interesting. They gradually climbed through Colorado. Near Aspen, they saw about forty miles of condominiums. They looked at the mining scars on the sides of the steep mountains. The weather in the mountains was about a month ahead of the weather back home on the Fond du Lac Reservation.

Luke looked at the green lodgepole pine and the yellow quaking aspen. The freeway followed every curve of the Colorado River. They reached ten thousand feet before they started to go downhill. Luke knew it was downhill because he began seeing runaway truck ramps. Some of them had been used recently.

"At one point, the freeway, the river, and the mountains came real close together," Luke said.

"Boy, that white man can build a road anywhere, can't he?"

The Rocky Mountains continued to amaze the flatland Indians. At one spectacular view, Luke was moved to say, "Way to go, God."

He wondered where that expression came from; then he remembered. It was from a Ziggy cartoon. The view kept changing as they continued west. It got to the point where they abbreviated it.

"Look over there, there's another WTGG."

"Yup, way to go, God."

Luke and Dave had both driven the van and were tired. It was Paneqwe's turn. Dave crawled in the back and Luke fell asleep in the front seat.

He woke up when there was a particularly loud crash of thunder. The van was swaying around the corners on the rain-slick mountain road. The windshield wipers were working when they wanted to.

Paneqwe was drinking coffee, snapping her gum loud, and

smoking a cigarette. She was hunched over the steering wheel; her knuckles were white where they bent around the wheel.

"Maybe if you slowed down a bit, it wouldn't be as scary," Luke told his wife.

She slowed down and began to relax as she drove down the mountain into the deserts of Utah and Arizona.

Luke and Paneqwe started talking about Las Vegas right after they crossed the Nevada state line. Dave must have overheard them because he sat up and said, "I've got another plan. Let's spend the night in Las Vegas. We can get up early and still be on time for your test."

"Is this the reason we came this way?" said Luke, as he remembered the stories about Dave and his love of gambling.

"Could be," confessed Dave.

He then told them of the many times he won thousands of dollars gambling in Las Vegas.

Luke and Paneqwe got a motel room. Dave didn't need one because he was going to gamble all night. After they showered and changed, Luke and Paneqwe went out to eat.

They were walking back to the motel when they decided to try their luck in a casino. The two Sawyer Indians sampled all the games of chance. After keno, video poker, slots, and roulette, they decided they liked the blackjack tables the best.

Luke quickly spent his gambling allowance. Paneqwe was doing good on the table. They left the casino when she was a couple of hundred dollars ahead.

The next morning, they checked out and waited by the van to meet Dave. Luke saw Dave swaggering down the street.

"How'd you do?" Luke asked.

"I got $4,700 here," he said as he pulled out a wad of greenbacks. All the bills in the wad looked like fifties.

"Good, let's go then. I've got to take a test and then get back home to finish making rice," said Luke.

"You drive. I've got to get some sleep," said Dave as he crawled in the back of the van.

Luke drove from Las Vegas through the Mojave Desert.

As they passed over a bridge, Luke asked Paneqwe, "Do you know why the fish in the Mojave River wear goggles?"

"No, why do they wear goggles?"

"To keep the sand out of their eyes," said Luke, pointing with his lips at the dry riverbed.

When they came down the mountains near San Bernardino, they saw a layer of something in the air.

"Is that fog?" she asked.

"No, I think it's smog."

"Remember what the air is like back home?" she asked.

"Yup, try not to breathe while we're in Los Angeles," he advised.

They wandered the freeways for a while. Eventually they found the off-ramp they were looking for. Eventually they found the TV station where the *Jeopardy!* test was administered. Luke had allowed plenty of dumb time to find the place. The dumb time was used up by the time they found a parking place.

Luke got out and waited by the studio gate. A line began to form behind him. There were about sixty people in line. He was the only one who wasn't white, the only Indian.

A contest coordinator came out and took charge.

"Welcome to the preliminary screening for *Jeopardy!* contestants," he California-smiled as he addressed the hopeful. Luke could tell he had done this many times before.

The coordinator ushered them into the actual soundstage used for the *Jeopardy!* program. Luke was slightly disappointed to see that Alex Trebek wasn't there.

The soundstage looked familiar, then Luke remembered that he had seen it about 250 times on his TV back home. He noted the applause sign for the studio audience. Off to one side of the set was a director's chair. The red chair was labeled Alex Trebek. Well, at least I get to see where he parks his ass between takes, Luke thought.

The coordinator passed out answer sheets and warned the hopeful that this was a difficult test. The hopeful watched a prerecorded tape. The questions came at ten-second intervals. There were fifty questions in fifty categories. Luke made a mark for each question he wasn't sure of. After the last question, the answer sheets were gathered up. They watched a *Jeopardy!* tape while the tests were being graded. The sixty hopeful were yelling out questions at the TV set.

The contest coordinator came back and called six names. He thanked the fifty-four hopeless for their time and effort. The losers trooped out of the building, including Luke.

Paneqwe and Dave were waiting when Luke walked out. She could tell what had happened by looking at Luke's eyes.

"Well, how'd it go?" asked Dave.

"Half of nothing is nothing," answered Luke. "I wish they would have asked me questions I knew. There were nine out of fifty I missed. They don't tell you your score."

"What happens now?" asked Dave.

"Nothing, unless you want to try this trip again."

"I don't think so. I want to go to Las Vegas," said a disappointed Dave.

"What's the rush? Enjoy the money you got now. We could play tourist here in Hollywood."

"No, I'm going to double my money when I get there."

When they got to Las Vegas, Luke got a motel room again. Dave rushed off after arranging a meeting place for the next morning. He had a gambler's gleam in his eye as he walked fast to the nearest casino.

Paneqwe gambled at the blackjack tables again. She was winning slowly but steadily. When she noticed a losing streak, she changed tables. Luke gambled big at the roulette and blackjack tables. He ran out of money real quick. He stood around and watched his wife win. She was more than five hundred dollars ahead when she quit.

They went to another casino that was offering a prime rib dinner for $2.99. Luke played keno while they were eating. He was using money he borrowed from Paneqwe. He didn't win.

The next morning they found Dave waiting outside the

motel. He looked sad. His pockets were turned inside out. Luke could tell he hadn't won.

"Well, how'd it go?" asked Luke, being polite.

"I was ten thousand dollars ahead," mumbled Dave.

"Was? Did you spend it all?"

"All of it. I was trying to stay up with the high rollers."

"Gas money too?" asked Luke.

"All of it. I don't know how we're getting home. I called a couple of people to send money, but it doesn't sound too hopeful," explained a chastened Dave.

"How are you going to get us home?" asked Luke.

"I don't know," he told the sidewalk.

Luke didn't tell him about Paneqwe's luck at the black-jack table. After all, it was Dave's responsibility to get them to *Jeopardy!* and back.

Dave went to a pay phone and tried calling his wife. She wouldn't accept his collect call. He slammed the phone down.

He talked about pawning his van. He said he would buy the Warmwaters a bus ticket home.

"Wonderful. Blow into town with a two-thousand-dollar van and leave town in a forty-thousand-dollar bus," said Luke.

After he pawned his van, Dave planned on winning enough to get it back out of hock. He planned on winning enough for gas money, he planned on winning enough for food. He planned on winning enough to buy Las Vegas presents for his wife and kids.

When he checked, he realized he didn't have the title for the van. He couldn't hock the truck.

"I've got fifty dollars she won. Do you want to eat or go back in and win what you lost?" asked Luke.

"I'll take that fifty and turn it into a couple of thousand," bragged Dave. He took the money and dashed into the nearest casino. Luke and Paneqwe waited outside.

Dave came out after a few minutes. He was walking slow.

"All of it?" asked Luke.

"All of it. They cleaned me out again. I can't believe it."

"Well, how do we get home now?" asked Luke.

"I don't know. I'll try calling my wife again," Dave told the sidewalk.

She wouldn't accept his call. He slammed the phone down. He went looking for his friend who worked at a casino. He couldn't find him, no answer on his phone either.

Dave checked at the Western Union to see if any of his previous pleas had been answered. They hadn't.

Finally, when Dave started talking about robbing one of the high-tolling winners, Luke told him that Paneqwe had enough money to get home. They left Las Vegas.

The trip home was grim. Dave was angry because they hadn't told him about the money. The Warmwaters were upset with Dave because he didn't pay their way home as promised. Luke and Paneqwe played cribbage through four states.

The Warmwaters bailed out when the van got to Minneapolis. They went to Luke's sister and asked for a ride home. She fed them and laughed at their Las Vegas story.

When they got home, they began to make rice gain. Another yearly cycle was ending. The birch and popple leaves were now on the ground.

"We've got about four batches left to finish," said Luke.

"Is the VCR watching *Jep* for us?"

"Yup, we can clean rice while we watch it."

"I'm glad to be home," she said as she eye-thanked him.

"Are we going to stop in Las Vegas next time?"

"Next time? When are we going out there again?" she asked.

"I made another appointment in January for *Jeopardy!*" he laughed.

"This time we're not going with Dave."

ADDITIONAL MATERIALS

INTRODUCTION
TO ADDITIONAL MATERIALS

The following words are from an alternative world called reality. The poems translated into Ojibwe are from an ongoing work in progress. I believe that Ojibwe elder who said, "With the language you are Anishinaabe, without it you are descendants of the Anishinaabe." The political columns are from the opinion pages of the *Duluth News Tribune* and were written in the early 1990s. My friend and relative, Jimmy Jackson, told me we should tell our own stories, so I did. The play, *Shinnob Jep*, has been performed over twenty times in various locations in Minnesota and Wisconsin, and once in Arkansas. The Northrup Road Players are ready to do it again anywhere.

Jim Northrup, 2013

INDIAN ISSUES: 1993

Wednesday, January 27, 1993, 6A
Blatant Racism Easier to Face than Closet Bigotry

As an Anishinaabe in northern Minnesota, I feel racism almost every day. It comes in many shades and variations. The examples I am relating are not the worst ones; they are just a reminder that one cannot really escape the ugliness.

A few years back, I was bringing my son home from the babysitter. He was in his car seat, and I stopped for a traffic light in downtown Duluth.

I saw a car pull up in the lane next to mine. I was looking at my son when I felt like someone was staring at me. I glanced up and saw a white woman in the next lane quickly look away. She then surreptitiously locked her car doors. I told my son to lock his doors.

I wondered who had more reason to be scared.

Once I wanted to buy a jacket. I had studied the ads and knew exactly what kind I wanted. It was made of Gore-Tex and would be used during three seasons of the year.

I went to a department store just off the reservation. I found the jacket I wanted. I was trying to decide on the color when I felt someone grab my arm.

The white store clerk had my sleeve pinched between her fingers and was trying to lead me off. While pulling she told me the cheaper jackets were at the end of the rack.

I pulled free and told the clerk I could afford the jacket. I then asked her to guess if I would buy a jacket from that store. I found another store where the clerk didn't judge my wallet by my skin color. I got the jacket and respect I wanted.

One payday evening, I took my family out to eat. While waiting for the hostess to seat us, we noticed everyone was staring. The people had stopped eating to look at us.

Everyone—old people, young people, babies in highchairs—they were all looking at us.

I did a quick check. All the members of my family were wearing clothes. We decided the white people were staring because we are Anishinaabe.

I put my index finger on my head and swiveled around. I gave them a 360-degree view of this Anishinaabe. It must have embarrassed them because they quickly went back to eating. We could feel eyes on us for the rest of the meal. It was a stare-down contest. We won because we had more experience with racism.

I have been to the boat landings and witnessed the fury of racism there. "Save Two Walleye, Spear A Pregnant Squaw" signs let me know precisely how these white people feel. It is almost refreshing to see people acting like they really feel. Blatant racism is always easier to face than closet bigotry.

Closet bigots smile hard at every Indian they meet. The false face doesn't quite hide the way they really feel. We often hear the jokes and comments made when they think no one is listening.

Closet bigots are everywhere. They can be found in business, in government, in education.

The closet bigots can be found in the media.

I sometimes shudder when I read in this newspaper how the "North Dakota Fighting Sioux beat the UMD Dogs." I wince when our tribal names are mispronounced on TV. I change stations when I hear jokes about Indians on the radio.

The phrase "level playing field" is now the latest buzzword that is used to put a veil on racism.

If we continue to allow racist labels and actions, if we continue to make human beings mascots, we all suffer.

I do not believe all white people are bigots, closet or otherwise. I know too many fine people who are not like that.

It is my hope that education and mutual understanding can change racial attitudes. We need to respect each other. We have a long way to go, but it's only been five hundred years.

We have made some progress. The United States and its citizens are no longer shooting at us.

Maybe I shouldn't have told my son to lock the door.

Wednesday, February 24, 1993, 4A
Mille Lacs Band Should Not Sell Treaty Rights

Voters from the Mille Lacs Reservation will decide whether to sell their 1837 treaty rights to the state of Minnesota. I think it is a bad deal for all who are involved in the sale.

It is similar to the situation Fond du Lac Reservation voters faced in 1988.

At Fond du Lac, we were informed by our tribal government that they were negotiating with the state regarding our 1854 treaty. We were told about the treaty sale after the agreement was written and signed.

A lot of Anishinaabeg don't think treaty rights should be sold. We think the rights belong to the generations to come. Our children, grandchildren, and their grandchildren should be able to use the treaties. The rights are ours to use while we are here, but ultimately they belong to future Anishinaabeg. We can't deny them their birthright. We can't sell something that belongs to them.

In our 1988 troubles, the tribal government persisted and sold our rights for one year. It was difficult to even get to vote on the issue.

We lobbied the Minnesota Legislature, we testified before the federal court, and petitioned twice for a referendum. We were blocked at every turn by our leaders, who were blinded by the money the state was dangling. Our leaders promised all sorts of good things would come out of the treaty sale. One promise was to use the money to build a war chest to protect treaty rights. Another promise was jobs for reservation people. The one-time payment was used to pay off old bills and loans. No new jobs were created and the war chest remains empty.

Fond du Lac people voted the treaty sale down twice. Our leaders learned there are some things more important than money. The leaders who sold the treaty rights are no longer in office. The lawyers who advised them are no longer working in Fond du Lac.

The state thinks it can get rid of the problem by throwing money around. Even if the sale of the 1837 treaty is successful at Mille Lacs, the state hasn't bought everyone's rights.

Anishinaabeg from Leech Lake, St. Croix, La Pointe, Lac Courte Oreilles, Lac du Flambeau, Sandy Lake, Red Lake, Red Cedar Lake, Gull Lake-Swan River, and Fond du Lac still have the right to hunt, fish, and gather in the 1837 ceded territory.

I wonder how the state would react if Anishinaabeg from other bands showed up at Mille Lacs to spear this spring? Would they make a federal case out of it? I'm sure the Anishinaabeg would be willing.

According to US Judge Barbara Crabb in Wisconsin, Anishinaabeg are entitled to 50 percent of the natural resources. That case involved the same 1837 treaty and was settled after a seventeen-year legal fight. The judge reaffirmed what we have been saying all along—Anishinaabeg have treaty rights.

The State of Wisconsin lost that case and had to pay for the lawyers used by the Anishinaabeg.

The treaty sale is a bad deal for the voting taxpayers of Minnesota. Spending $10 million in these days of budget deficits doesn't make economic sense. The money spent will not end the treaty rights troubles.

Now I am wondering why the Mille Lacs band is so willing to sell its share of the 1837 treaty. I am also wondering why they are trying to make the non-Indian anglers happy. The recent concessions make it seem like Mille Lacs is negotiating from a position of weakness rather than strength. Did Bud Grant and his cronies win? What kind of a sale is it when the buyer tells the seller how to spend the money? What is the gambling connection? Does the Mille Lacs band have a gambling compact knife held to its throat?

It looks like Mille Lacs is letting the threats of racists determine their future. Wisconsin boat landing tactics are used as an excuse to sell treaties.

A lot of Anishinaabeg know that treaties will last longer than casinos.

Wednesday, March 24, 1993, 6A
Indian Gambling Shifts Money, Not Prejudice

What was life like on the Indian reservation before gambling? Let's go back to 1980 and take a look.

Indians were facing discrimination and prejudice on a daily basis. Bigots were everywhere. The towns around the reservations were the worst. I called it a hate circle around the "rez."

Most Americans were not aware of the problems Indians faced every day. Their view of us was a mix of nineteenth century idealism and twentieth century Hollywood. Some people were even surprised that we were still here. We learned how to survive the racism that surrounded us. We taught our children, also.

The system's tentacles reached deeper into our lives than any other population group. Once an Indian got wrapped up, it was difficult to escape. Indians were not people; they were clients, patients, or inmates—sometimes lumped together and called a caseload.

The probation officer talked to the judge who talked to the police who talked to the lawyer who talked to the social worker who talked to the counselor who talked to the child protection worker who talked to the probation officer. Indians enmeshed in the system rarely got away without losing their dignity, their freedom, or their children.

Jails always held more than their share of Indians. The sentences seemed to be longer and the punishments more severe. A jury of their peers was a joke. The Indians in the courtrooms either wore connected steel bracelets or were called defendants. Going to jail was considered normal and not an aberration. There were many family reunions in the cell blocks. It was tough being a free Indian in those days.

Schools added to the problem by labeling most Indian children as learning-disabled. Once a label was applied, it was hard to remove. In school, the children learned that they were "discovered" and were a "conquered people." They also learned the wisdom of the white man, with no mention of their own contributions.

White students were especially cruel to the Indians. My son told me it doesn't feel good to be called a dirty Indian in civics class. Some schools had Indians as mascots, something less than human. It was a challenging test to be an Indian in the schools then. It is no surprise that most students quit before graduation.

Foster homes and adoption agencies did a brisk business. The children were taken from their families at an alarming rate. Indians learned a new word: dysfunctional. The word meant someone else was going to raise your kids. It was sad to watch these born-Indian, raised-white people returning to the reservation. We helped them find the identity that was taken by the system. It was hard to even remain Indian back then.

Indian people exercising their reserved treaty rights were arrested by state game wardens. Wild rice, deer meat, ducks, and fish were confiscated. Canoes, nets, and guns were also taken. Every arrest and confiscation was a reminder of how the United States kept its word in the treaties. Indians continued to exercise their rights in spite of the arrests. They were the only ones who believed the words in the treaty. It was hard being a treaty-believing Indian in the early 1980s.

Back in the bad old days, tribal governments were trying to qualify for federal grants. Job training programs blossomed and then withered. A lot of us learned a little about a lot of different occupations. On my rez, we had welders, carpenters, heavy equipment operators, natural resources technicians, and electronics workers.

We followed the Golden Rule in those days—them that got the gold make the rules. Washington and foundation dollars ruled the reservations with their policies. Tribal governments were learning how to flex their economic muscles.

Here it is the '90s and nothing has changed except the calendar. We are still facing racism—personal and institutional. The only difference is tribal government now has control of the gambling gold.

Wednesday, April 28, 1993, 6A
Almost an Elder: Reflections on Turning Fifty

I am about to celebrate my 50th birthday. I suppose it is quite common to reflect on what has happened in those fifty years.

I am finally at the age where it doesn't matter if my belly bulges a bit. No matter how many sit-ups I do, the bulge is still there. I did one just the other day, and it didn't change a thing.

When I was young, I used to hear the average age of death for Indians was forty-four years. I adopted an attitude that anything over that many years was pure gravy, just juice. It was a bonus for trying to live a good life.

I was born during World War II. I remember my grandmother, Angeline, taking me to downtown Duluth to watch the victory parade that signaled the end of that war. I recall my uncles, Rob, Stun, Ole, and Hayman, talking about exotic places like France, North Africa, and the South Pacific.

Shortly after the war, I was sent to a federal boarding school at Pipestone, Minnesota. I have blocked out most memories of that experience, but I do recall wondering why just Indians went away to school. I remember asking my mother, Alice, why white people didn't have to leave home when they were in the first grade. She couldn't answer; she just looked away, but not before I saw the pain in her eyes.

I was still in boarding school when the Korean War was

fought. My older cousin, Clarence Blacketter, came home and told stories about the war.

After high school, I joined the Marine Corps. I went through the Panama Canal during the Cuban Missile Crisis. We didn't invade Cuba and just visited Puerto Rico and Jamaica.

From there we went across the Pacific to practice war in Okinawa, Japan; Taiwan; and the Philippines. We were in Subic Bay when John Kennedy was killed.

In 1965, I went to Vietnam with the Third Marine Division. I spent thirteen months there during the war and returned to the reservation with my own war stories to tell.

My two oldest sons, James and Matthew, were born during the Vietnam War. I remember feeling they shouldn't have to fight in a war because I had done it. Nobody hates war as much as someone who has been in one. I was glad my sons were not in the military when the Marines were blown up in Lebanon. I worried for their future when the shooting was going on in Grenada and Panama.

My family suffered during the Persian Gulf War because Matthew was in the Army then. I was worried he might have to go fight. He didn't have to go, and I was relieved when it was over.

Now I have three grandsons: Aciigog, Mato, and Niiwin. At first I thought I was too young to be living with a grandmother. The years have changed my opinion. I used to look for my own grandfather when the children called me Grandpa. After hearing it for three years, I am beginning to identify myself as grandpa. For example, just the other day I grabbed Aciigog's hand and told him he could go to the store with Grandpa. I wonder what the future holds for them.

When I was in my physical prime, I used to start running and would be at top speed in a step or two. Over the years I have noticed that it takes longer and longer to get up to full speed. Right now it takes about an hour and a half to get there.

By that time I have forgotten why I wanted to run in the first place. As I get older, I find fewer reasons to run at full speed. Now that I am getting closer to becoming an elder, I look around and see all the things I have yet to learn. I am hoping to learn from my elders and my grandchildren. I can hardly wait to see what the next fifty years brings. Wouldn't it be nice to be old enough to say anything you want?

Wednesday, May 26, 1993, 8A
Mille Lacs Spearing Challenge Will Test Rights

In Mille Lacs County my last name is "Defendant." With some other Anishinaabeg, I was cited for possessing a spear on Mille Lacs Lake. We were charged with violating a Minnesota law that prohibits spear fishing before May 1.

We were using our 1837 treaty rights to hunt, fish, and gather in the ceded territory.

This was not a spur-of-the-moment idea. For many months, Anishinaabeg have been watching the treaty sellout that was being negotiated between the Mille Lacs Band of Ojibwe and the State of Minnesota.

There are many Anishinaabeg who believe treaty rights are not ours to sell. The rights are ours to use and protect while we're here, but, ultimately, they belong to the generations to come. How can we sell our children's birthright?

Anishinaabeg from what are now called Michigan, Wisconsin, and Minnesota had been meeting for several months to discuss selling treaty rights. The meetings led to the formation of a group called the Anishinaabe Liberation Front.

We had a couple of reasons for calling our group that name. First, it makes people aware that we are Anishinaabe. By calling ourselves that, we force the media to use the word Anishinaabe over and over. Second, some liked the humor of that little orange character on the TV comedy "Alf." That demonstrates how Anishinaabeg use humor as a survival mechanism.

There is no one leader of ALF—we make decisions by consensus. We decided to spear at Mille Lacs to show everyone that we don't think treaties should be sold.

We ran the gauntlet of media people when we met in East Lake to plan our night's spear fishing. There were five satellite TV trucks and more microphones than spears.

Late in the afternoon, one newspaper person wanted to know what the holdup was; why we were not out at Mille Lacs? We told her that we usually wait until after dark before we go spearing. It makes the fish easier to see.

We went to Agate Bay on Mille Lacs Lake. We chose that part of the lake because we were cooperating with the Aitkin County sheriff as we staged our symbolic spearing. In fact, the sheriff came to an ALF meeting to make sure the event would be peaceful. We let him know we were not radicals or terrorists but merely Anishinaabe people who believed in treaty rights.

At Agate Bay as the first cars of the fifty-car convoy stopped, we heard gunfire. We notified conservation officers, who called the sheriff. Because we did not want to jeopardize anyone's safety, we moved to our alternate site.

At the Cedar Creek landing, the state officials and the Mille Lacs County deputies were waiting. Some of us actually got out on the lake. We offered tobacco to thank the creator. A state Department of Natural Resources boat came up and officials inspected our canoe. They didn't see the spear, and when I asked them if we were under arrest, they said no. We paddled away and began looking for fish.

I stood up with my light and spear and began looking at the lake bottom. Initially I didn't see any fish. I did see a lot of un-recycled trash down there. There were plastic bags, beer and soda cans, a padlock, and some stuff I couldn't identify.

I began to see fish, but before I could spear any, the DNR officers turned on their spotlight and motored over to our canoe. This time they found the spear and issued a citation. They confiscated my light and spear and gave me a receipt.

The conservation officers advised me of my court date and told me that, if I were found guilty, my spear and light would be sold at a public auction. The officers were polite and professional as they carried out their duties. We were also polite and professional as we carried out our treaty rights duties.

So now I am facing a $700 fine and ninety days in jail if found guilty. Our legal defense team is doing research on the issue and representing us in court. I believe we will win like the Anishinaabeg in Wisconsin did in the Voigt case.

As I wait for my next court date, I wonder what is the difference between using a light and spear to gather fish and using an electronic fish locator. Maybe Alf knows.

Wednesday, June 23, 1993, 6A
New Black Bear Casino Benefits Indians, Others

The Bear is up and running. Tribal Chairman Sonny Peacock calls the new Black Bear Casino an economic shot in the arm for the Fond du Lac Reservation and the surrounding community. Some Chippewa people call it Makade-Makwa.

The $15 million to $18 million (estimates vary) Black Bear Casino had what Peacock seductively called a soft opening. This is what the Navy calls a shakedown cruise. The grand entry for the casino will be on the July 4th holiday.

Fonjalackers are invited for the doings on July 1. The casino calls it Fond du Lac Days. There will be prizes and giveaways.

The Bear is at the intersection of Highway 210 and I-35. It brings to mind the old saying about real estate—the three most important things to remember are location, location, and location.

Peacock is betting that the customers will pour off the freeway to pour money into the slot machines. The fact that the Bear is wholly owned by the reservation means we will not be splitting the profits with some outside management company or city. Peacock says any Fond du Lac Band member can get a job at the casino.

Personally, I have a long list of relatives and friends working there. The steady paychecks are contributing to their self-esteem. Two sisters, a couple of nieces, and a lot of cousins are cashing paychecks from the casino.

As an Anishinaabe walking around the new casino, I think it is sort of funny that the customers think all Indians are employees of the Bear. I gave directions to the restrooms three times before I could get my first quarter in one of the machines.

The big round building is clean, bright, and easy on the eyes. Parking is easy even without the free valet service. Casino employees were everywhere to answer questions or provide service to the customers. There will be examples of Anishinaabe art on the walls when the decorating is done. Jeff Savage had a hand in selecting the art. I bet his wife, Sandy, helped.

There were a few problems to be worked out in the new building. Not all the advertised 1,000 slots are hooked up yet. The ones that were working made a pleasant boing, boing sound as people bet their money. Boing, boing—more money for Fond du Lac; boing, boing—more money for Fond du Lac. At some of the slot machines, I saw gamblers playing for a new red Jeep or a boat and motor.

The food is being served from a tent on the west side of the building until the inside place is ready to go. The price of the food makes me take two steps back—$4.50 for a hot dog? The price would be OK if the plate was filled with Perch Lake rice and a couple of pieces of fry bread. Real fry bread, not that frozen bread dough stuff. I would pay $4.50 for a hot dog like that.

While gazing around, I noticed that the majority of the gamblers had gray hair—sort of like that bumper sticker that says: "We are spending our children's inheritance."

I imagine someone has already done a study on the typical casino customer on Indian reservations.

I saw the bingo hall when I rode the escalator upstairs. I can hardly wait to give bingo a try. I was one of the first bingo hall employees when the reservation began gambling operations. That was in the days when players slid a plastic window over the numbers and bought the cards a dime at a time. It was a nickel and dime operation compared to this multi-million dollar business.

The current Reservation Business Committee should be commended for their work in putting the Bear together. Don Soderberg and Gary Harms should also be recognized for their planning. We better not forget anyone else who helped make the casino a reality. That means the Shinnob who carried the blocks when they were just building. It also includes the maintenance people who clean up, the slot machine fixers, the change venders, the slot supervisors, the security people, the blackjack dealers, the pit bosses, the parking valets, and the customers.

The Black Bear Casino contributes to integration of the races. I smile when I see white people reaffirming tribal sovereignty a quarter at a time.

Boing, boing.

Wednesday, July 28, 1993, 8A
Border an Invisible Barrier to Chippewa

In the old days, the settlers would start getting nervous right about now: two thousand Indians are gathering.

The gathering will be held on August 5th in International Falls and Fort Frances from 1 to 3:30 PM.

The plans call for two thousand First Nation people to come together—one thousand Chippewa from the United States and one thousand Chippewa from Canada. That is a lot of Indians all in one place. My family is going because we have never seen two thousand Chippewa all at one time.

It's an easy day to remember: it's on a Thursday and the day before the Mash-Ka-Wisen powwow in Sawyer. There will be three drums from Canada, including the Whitefish Bay Singers. The Kingbird Singers from Minnesota will be there too. So will the Bois Forte Traditional Drum and the Vermillion Young Eagles. For those interested in the power of songs and singing, this is the place to be.

The event is being coordinated by the Minnesota Chippewa and Canadian Chippewa tribes. Planning has been going on for months. Faxes have been crossing the international border like it wasn't even there.

Darrell "Chip" Wadena, president of the Minnesota Chippewa Tribe, has stated, "It is important that we show support to enforce and uphold the treaties recognizing the rights that indigenous people have in respect to international borders, freedom of movement, exemptions from customs, and other rights."

The Tribal Executive Committee will be meeting in International Falls next Wednesday so Minnesota tribal leaders will be in town for the rally.

Chippewa have been making sandwiches, arranging for medical and media coverage, and lining up transportation. Chippewa on both sides of the imaginary line have been preparing the spiritual and traditional gifts they are going to exchange.

The gift bundles will contain wild rice, smoked fish, tobacco, sweet grass, and sage.

The drums will lead the Canadian Chippewa across the border where they will rally with the Minnesota Chippewa at Smokey Bear Park in International Falls. The two groups will then return to the border, where they are going to exchange gifts. Tribal leaders will present US and Canadian customs representatives a declaration of rights from participating tribes. Both groups will cross the bridge and go into Canada. The US tribes will walk back across the border at the conclusion of the rally.

That is the plan unless someone snags it up and decides to stay on one side of the line or the other. Rain or shine, the rally will go on. Rain might even be helpful to let the world know how determined the Chippewa people are.

One part of the get-together is to commemorate the Jay Treaty. This is the one that calls for the freedom of movement of indigenous people between the Canadian and United States border.

Two contact people have been identified: Bonnie Lowe, whose numbers are (voice) (218) 335-8586, (fax) (218) 335-6562; and Joanne Belisle, (voice) 1-800-665-3384, (fax) (807) 548-5041.

My family has had some personal experience with US Customs. A couple of years ago, we were coming back from Winnipeg when we were stopped at the United States border. Our car had Fond du Lac Reservation plates.

The man with the gun told us to pull our car off to the side and come into the building. He told us to leave the car keys in the car. Once inside, my wife, Patricia, son, Joseph, and I were taken to separate rooms. We surrendered our identification papers. The first gun was joined by another gun blocking the door. Joseph and I emptied our pockets on the table and removed our moccasins at their order.

It was like a scene from a bad Gestapo movie. It sure didn't feel like the United States. It was like we had to prove we were not crooks or bad guys. I thought a body cavity search was next. They let us go and we were quiet for the next fifty miles.

I will be part of the rally so I don't have to worry about where someone wants to search.

Wednesday, August 25, 1993, 8A
Cool Mornings Harbingers of Wild Rice Harvest

The cool of the August mornings let me know that ricing is almost here. Ricing is the annual gift from the Creator to the Anishinaabeg and others.

When Indian people meet on the road, at the bingo hall, or in the clinic, the conversation usually ends up about ricing. Great ricing stories are beginning to be retold.

One of my favorites is the time some Indians sold a rice buyer something other than rice. They added a couple of rocks to increase the weight of the rice. The next day, the rice buyer came back and sold the Indians some groceries. The Indians found the same rocks in their flour. Like most stories, this one could be five minutes or five hours long depending on the skill of the storyteller. The story has a timeless quality about it. It apparently happened in the 1930s or '40s.

The power of the story comes from our reaction. One person could hear the story from a moral point of view and reaffirm his belief that cheaters never prosper. Another could listen to the same story and say: "Well, we tried to trick that white man and it didn't work. We'll have to come up with a better one than that."

A third could just hear nothing beyond a ricing story. That one would take a mind trip back to when they were ricing. The flood of memories would bring a smile to that listener.

Someone else would say: "Hey, wait a minute. He stole my best story about the rocks and rice."

A businessman might say, "What the hey. The guy still made money. The rocks were more valuable as rice than as flour."

"I remember my dad telling this story" would be another response as that listener went back in family history and recalled her dad laughing as he retold the same story.

I listen to and tell ricing stories.

As a lifelong fry bread-propelled ricer, I am looking forward to that first time out on the lake. In addition to the rice, I might just find a new story there. I will offer tobacco like I'm supposed to before I harvest the gift.

I checked the knockers used in brushing rice. The kids didn't play sword fighter with them this year so they are ready to go. The brownish cedar is worn smooth from years of brushing the rice plants. My hands curl around them like Lee Trevino with his sweetest putter, maybe like Kirby Puckett with a bat.

The rice pole feels strong. The diamond willow fork that took two winters to carve looks ready. The spruce pole I got from my cousin is springy. I'm ready to rice.

There is someone I met who is not ready for ricing. She will be attending a four-day workshop on wild rice. It is to be held up near Ely. When she was telling me about the workshop, it sounded like one of those mystical BWCA kind of experiences. They will be making ricing poles and knockers, harvesting, parching, and dancing on the rice. Then they will fan it and eat the product of their labor. All of this in four days. She didn't say if she would get continuing education credits for the wild rice project.

As an interested ricer, I asked what she was going to use to get the rice beards out of her eye. She asked: "What are rice beards?"

The Minnesota Department of Natural Resources will make their usual announcement about the opening of the season. Some of us suspect that a dart and calendar are used to set the dates.

While these preparations are going on, the highway vendors will still be there, peddling their black paddy product and calling it wild rice. The vendors have been fooling the tourists all summer with their cheap, manufactured product that is anything but wild.

The wild rice season means a lot of things to different people. As for me and my family, we know exactly what ricing means. The cool August mornings tell me to make sure I'm ready for the Creator's gift.

Wednesday, September 22, 1993, 6A
Wild Rice Harvest Connects Family Generations

Ricing was good this year for our family. Harvesting wild rice is one of our favorite seasonal activities. Turning the wild rice into food gives us a chance to do what our parents and grandparents did at this time of the year. We know their parents and grandparents made rice also. We feel connected.

In this era of machines, we still make rice the way the old people did. In an economics class many years ago, I learned the way we make rice is called labor intensive. We just call it a lot of hard work.

First, the rice must be harvested. We go to the area lakes and rivers to gather rice. In spite of the many doom and gloom predictions of a bad year for wild rice, we found enough for our needs.

For a while, everyone was a wild rice expert. It was common knowledge that the rice crop was bad this year. If I had one person tell me the crop was bad, I had twenty-five people saying that. Unfortunately, most of the people talking about the bad crop have never spent a day on the lake ricing. It is so much easier to talk about ricing than it is to actually do it.

While out on the lake, we saw many of the same animals that are in zoos. We saw eagles, ducks, coots, otters, muskrats, and a bear.

As long-time ricers, we know how important it is to clean the rice of debris. Rice heads, leaves, lily pads, and moose ears are constantly removed from the wild rice. Once we got the rice sacked up and the canoe loaded, we came home and spread the rice out in the sun to dry.

I showed my thirteen-year-old son, Joseph, how I like to build the fire under the parching kettle. He split wood while learning.

My wife, Pat, and I took turns parching the rice. The smell of the fire and parching rice spread from our backyard. A friend tried to compare the smell of parching rice to something. He quit when we told him it smelled like parching rice. We paddled many miles in that black kettle.

Pat set up her dancing pit. She used her clean, handmade moccasins to grind the hulls off the wild rice. A pleasing sound came from the pit as she moved her feet.

While fanning, we watched the rice turn from the brown of the hulls to the green of the rice. The fanner moved around with the wind so the hulls would blow away.

Our grandson, Aaron, played while we worked. He learned not to get too close to the fire. He learned not to stand downwind while we were fanning the rice. Aaron taught us that he liked to eat rice out of the fanning basket. We gave him a choice between rice and a candy bar. He chose the rice.

This was Joseph's first time out on the lake ricing. This season was his first as a ricer.

Joe learned how to pole the canoe from the front. At one point he wanted to quit, but we were out in the lake, so he couldn't. Joe finally got the hang of it and found the right speed for the knocker in the back of the canoe. After watching other ricers and his dad, Joe got a chance to knock rice. He got advice from some of his elders.

When we got home, Joe built the fire and parched our day's harvest. By the fourth batch, he knew when to take the rice out of the kettle. I decided to give him the rice we gathered that day. Next he will use Pat's dancing pit to loosen the hulls. After that he will fan it and clean it. He will then have about twenty pounds of hand-finished rice.

Once again, ricing was a media event. Channel 9 from the Twin Cities was there to record Joe's first time at ricing. They didn't come for the family event; we were just out ricing when they showed up. A magazine called *Martha Stewart Living* sent out an art director and photographer from New York to record the labor-intensive process of turning wild rice into food.

The Creator gave us food again. We know what lake our rice comes from. We even know what part of the lake it grew in. The family members now have new ricing stories to tell.

Only eleven more months until ricing again.

Wednesday, November 24, 1993, 8A
Reservation Business Session Brings Questions

There was a paper turkey hanging above the Fond du Lac Reservation Business Committee. The Thanksgiving decoration slowly spun as the meeting began. It was the monthly open meeting of the RBC, our tribal government.

It is where Fonjalackers can talk with the leaders. The meeting was held at the ex-casino/blackjack school building in Cloquet. The people sit in rows of chairs facing the tables occupied by RBC members.

The meeting vaguely followed Bob's Rules. I don't know where the pipe ceremony fits in Roberts Rules of Order. I wondered why we were having the ceremony. How many people there believe in the pipe?

Chairman Sonny Peacock opened the meeting and began following the printed agenda. The various directors stood up and said they had nothing further to add to their reports. I couldn't find any reports, so I didn't know what they were talking about. The directors who were too busy sent their underlings to say they had nothing to add to the reports.

The meeting got lively when Fonjalackers started asking questions. Some questions were directed at the directors and some went to the RBC.

A Fonjalacker wanted to know about $400,000 that was transferred from the education division. The same questioner wanted to have a referendum on the need for a new school.

A question from the audience was directed at the RBC. The Fonjalacker wanted to know why the rez lawyer was living in a rez HUD house. The chairman said the rez lawyer has a home in Duluth.

The meeting moved on to questions about the casino. One Fonajalacker wanted to know who had access to the daily slot machine report. Secretary-Treasurer Pete Defoe said he uses it in the course of his duties. The subject of RBC members gambling at the casino came up. George Dupuis,

RBC member, said what he does after business hours is his own business. He further stated that if it bothered people so much he would quit gambling there. Dupuis also is on the Board of Management, Inc., which oversees gaming on the Fond du Lac Reservation.

The rez is going into the newspaper business. At least that is what they are calling it. Mike LeGarde, the current editor of the *Fond du Lac News,* says they are going to be printing sixteen to twenty-four pages monthly. The new publication will be out at the first of the year. It will be distributed free to all Fond du Lac Band members.

LeGarde answered questions about the new venture. Most of the questions centered around whether the new publication would be a real newspaper or just a house organ of the RBC.

One Fonjalacker wanted to know whether a letter to the editor critical of the RBC would be printed. Both the editor and Chairman Peacock talked around the question for a while.

When they were done talking, they hadn't answered the question.

Toward the end of the chairman's monologue about freedom of the press and other issues, he said: "You will have the right to express an opinion, but someone might get angry and harassment might follow."

I sat in amazement, listening to our proponent of democracy say that if we used our freedoms we might get harassed. The chairman was adamant that this was a true newspaper as long as it prints positive things about the RBC.

When asked why a Fonjalack-owned print shop was not hired to print the new rez news, LeGarde replied, "He can't print the pictures in color."

The new publication values color over objectivity, flash instead of truth. George Mason was right when he said: "Freedom of the press is one of the great bulwarks of liberty, and it can never be restrained but by despotic governments."

That seemed like a good place for the Reservation Business Committee to live up to its name. They had a chance to do something good, and they did nothing. If the new Fonjalacker can't print in color because he needs a new press, they could have helped him with a business loan. Yet, we see how quick they are to spend money on casino business.

The meeting slowly came to an end. The RBC members walked off as Chairman Peacock continued answering questions from the Fonjalackers. The turkey kept on spinning.

Wednesday, December 22, 1993, 7A
Indian Gaming Exciting but May Eat Us

I have heard that gambling is called the new buffalo for the Indian people. I disagree with that comparison. I think gambling is a tiger. I also think gambling is like riding a tiger. It's an exciting ride, but how do we get off the tiger?

I know it is exciting when I go to the bingo hall or put my rolls of nickels in the slot machines.

According to Donald Trump, Indian casinos are ripe for a takeover by organized crime. In his testimony before Congress, Trump said the mob has already infiltrated casinos run by Indians. However, he could offer no proof other than everyone is talking about it.

Here on the Fond du Lac Reservation we don't have to worry about organized crime—it is the unorganized crime we have to worry about.

The original agreement with the City of Duluth that established the Fond du Luth Casino is an example. On the reservation we are wondering why we are giving away the casino profits. The National Indian Gaming Commission agreed and said that we are to get 70 percent instead of the 25 percent in the agreement.

The Rez and the city are trying to decide how to split the millions. Instead of a harmonious relationship, we have become adversaries. I expect one side or the other to make a federal case out of it. Meanwhile, the money will remain tied up and benefit no one but the bankers. Fond du Luth has been in operation for seven years, and I have yet to see a dime of the profits.

One of the selling points used was the promise of jobs for reservation members. When I go to Fond du Luth, all I see are non-Indians working there. If this is an Indian casino, where are the Indians?

The tiger doesn't care who it consumes. Remember an accountant we had here at Fond du Lac? He stole more than $60,000 of our money to feed the gambling tiger. His reputation and career were sacrificed to the tiger.

More recently, the area director of the Bureau of Indian Affairs, Earl Barlow, was suspended because he accepted gambling vouchers from one of the casinos he was regulating. His assistant was also suspended. That's two more careers for the gambling tiger.

Those are two of the highly publicized cases. We read of others who steal from their employers to feed the gambling tiger. Who will be corrupted next by gambling?

The Reservation Business Committee spends a lot of time, brainpower, and money on gambling. Chairman Peacock of the Fond du Lac Reservation recently estimated that he spends one-third of his time on gambling issues. I think his estimate was a little low. I bet it is 50 percent or more. That is a lot of effort for something that doesn't directly benefit the Indian people.

Gambling begets greed. The tiger is making us forget who we are as people. Gambling is teaching us not to share. Most tribal councils do not share the profits with the people. There are a few exceptions. The Mille Lacs Ojibwe people just got $500 each from their gambling.

The Lower Sioux are paying some of their tribal members a per capita payment. It is creating a class society because not all members get to share in the profits. Other Dakota people get a per capita payment. Only a small fraction of Indians actually get money from gambling.

Here at Fond du Lac we get a ham.

I don't think gambling contributes to racial harmony. Since the house always wins, there are more people walking out mad because they lost. I can just about picture the losers saying: "Those (dirty word, dirty word) Indians got all my money." Since the experience is negative, I don't see how they can think positive about Indians.

It is what gambling is doing to us as people we should be thinking about. We have survived on this continent for hundreds of generations because of our values and traditions. I don't think we can afford to make gambling a new Indian tradition.

I worry that we are becoming full-blooded members of the rat race. Values and traditions are more important than money. Will the gambling tiger get our sovereignty next?

INDIAN ISSUES: 1994

Wednesday, January 26, 1994, 7A
Black Bear Casino Layoffs Stressful to Indians

"Regrettably, for economic reasons, it is necessary to lay off a number of employees. This letter is to inform you that you are among the employees affected."

That was the beginning of the letter sent to some sixty Black Bear Casino employees. More than half of the people who got the letters were Indian.

A formula put together by gambling management was used to decide who to lay off. It was run on a point system that gave five points off for a no call-no show, four points off for an unexcused absence, three points off for being late or for an undocumented illness, two points off for other reasons, and finally one point off for a documented illness.

Needless to say the letter caused stress in the Indian community. The feeling was that, since it is our casino, why let white people decide who gets to work?

In a hastily called meeting, laid-off employees came to the Sawyer Center to talk about the event. In angry tones, the employees related what happened to them at work. One elderly Indian was told to go to hell by the chairman of the reservation during a phone call. Another spoke of scheduling problems. As a working mother, she has to work midnights while young, single white people work days. One employee was told the lay off was for two weeks, another was told two months.

Some Indians complained about white people being hired off the street and quickly becoming supervisors. When people complain about job conditions, management defers to the Reservation Business Committee, which points at management as the source of the problem. The people vented their anger and then decided to meet with the Reservation Business Committee as soon as possible.

At 9 AM the next day, the halls of the RBC building began to fill with Fond du Lac people. They were there to meet with their government, their leaders. The entire Reservation Business Committee was present. Chairman Sonny Peacock addressed the assembled Fond du Lac people and told them why the layoff occurred and what was used to determine who was to be laid off. He explained the formula used by gambling management and the RBC.

The laid-off Fond du Lac people listened to the explanation and then began to tell their chairman what was wrong. Various people described what was happening with them and their jobs. One security person said he was threatened by a customer with a gun. He was told to forget it because the customer gambled a lot. Another customer wanted her change from a white person only. One employee was sent home because the place wasn't busy. This was counted as an unexcused absence for her.

The meeting lasted for three hours. Secretary/Treasurer Pete Defoe told the people of some of the problems for the casino. He also said he understood that the Indian people are not being treated fairly. Defoe said it is his job to get the Fond du Lac people back to work. He promised that the complaints will not be ignored.

A Fond du Lac member said a new memo came out saying that if anyone talked about the layoff, they would be given three days off or be terminated.

Chairman Peacock was asked how many Indian and white employees there are at the casino. He said he didn't know. Peacock told the employees who were laid off they can protest the decision. He promised that each case would be reviewed by the Reservation Business Committee. He also warned the people that attendance standards would not be lowered.

The letter to the laid-off employees also said there was no guarantee of re-employment. It closed by saying: "Former employees are asked to refrain from gaming at the casino for a period of thirty days from the date of separation." The letter was signed by Dick Joki.

The RBC is now in a position where it has to choose between their people and their management.

No one asked the question of why the casino was "substantially overstaffed."

When will the promise of jobs for the Fond du Lac people become a reality? After all, it's our casino.

Wednesday, February 23, 1994, 7A
Paper Right in Expunging Indian Nicknames

It made it easier to kill Vietnamese people during the war if we called them gooks. We didn't see them as human beings; they weren't fathers, brothers, or sons. They were just a label.

And that shows the power of labeling.

The *Star Tribune* of Minneapolis decided not to use sports nicknames that are offensive to Indians.

In a recent column, Dominic Papatola, the *Duluth News-Tribune's* arts and entertainment writer and columnist, wrote that the Minneapolis paper was damaging its editorial credibility by refusing to print offensive nicknames. He calls it quibbling about semantics. I think he is carrying on an academic argument with himself. He is talking lofty concepts when he should be down in the gutter of reality.

It was not quibbling when my son was shown the tomahawk chop by his white classmates. They were chopping at his identity and self-esteem. That was racism learned directly from the sports teams. The cute symbol was used to deliver a brutal message of hate. The fact that it happened in civics class made it worse.

It is fortunate for the writer that he has not experienced racism on a daily basis. It makes it easier for him to stand on the outside and decide what is politically correct about racism.

He says education is the answer to changing offensive nicknames. Where has he been? There have been protests at the World Series and Super Bowl games. Indians were there to educate the fans about offensive nicknames. How much more educating do we have to do? Would yet another news release help?

Maybe the gambling casinos could use their economic clout to educate people about offensive nicknames. The casinos could band together and buy World Series-Super Bowl ad time. They could use their thirty seconds to promote mutual respect instead of offensive nicknames. On a local level they could only buy ad space in newspapers that don't use offensive labels.

That way they could be a part of the solution instead of propagating the attitudes that say it is good business to demean a race of humans.

Offensive nicknames are just one of the ugly faces of racism. Indians suffered at the boat landings when they were called timber niggers. The Hey-yah song used by the sports fans is particularly offensive.

Papatola is the keeper of the status quo. He thinks the Minneapolis newspaper has gone too far when it quits using racist labels.

I have always thought that newspapers were supposed to educate and inform. By taking such a strong stand, the Minneapolis newspaper is educating its readers to the reality of racist labels. It has informed them that offensive nicknames will not be used. The efforts should be applauded—the actions emulated. Way to go, *Star Tribune*.

The *Duluth News Tribune* doesn't use the "Fighting Sioux" and "Dogs" as much in the sports pages. Small changes are being made and felt.

Offensive nicknames are just that—offensive. By not using them, we go beyond being politically correct to showing mutual respect.

Fighting racism is a lifelong struggle for those who are impacted by it. Let's quickly review some US history. Some one hundred years ago the policy of shooting Indians was pretty much over. Indians became US citizens seventy years ago, and sixty years ago we got tribal governments. In the 1960s Indians got civil rights, in the '70s religious freedom. In the '80s we got gambling. From shooting to gambling in just a few generations. It has been long trail.

All of us want to make the trail easier for our children and grandchildren. Not using offensive nicknames would help.

It was a Chinese man, not a gook, who said the longest journey begins with a single step.

Wednesday, March 23, 1994, 7A
Store Nuclear Waste in Yards of NSP Officials

I think it is a dumb idea to store radioactive wastes on an island in the Mississippi River. Not only dumb but dangerous. Northern States Power has a plan to keep killer waste in dry casks at Prairie Island.

The company is mounting an impressive ad campaign in the usual media outlets. Expensive full-page ads and sound bites on TV are being used to persuade us it is OK to store the killer waste there. NSP wants the storage, so they can keep making more killer waste. We should be talking about conservation instead of generating more waste.

Minnesota legislators are debating the storage issue. The vote was yes and no in various committees. Now they are talking compromise. I don't think it's possible to compromise with killer waste. We must quit making things that are dangerous for ten thousand years.

The storage is supposed to be temporary until a permanent repository is built by the federal government. Earthquake-prone Yucca Mountain in Nevada has been suggested as one such place. The Mescalero Apache of New Mexico are saying they will build a private storage site for nuclear waste on their reservation. It is private because the affected state is against the idea. Ruffina Laws, a Mescalero Apache, is speaking out against the idea.

The idea of storing killer waste in a flood plain flies in the face of logic. We still have not recovered from that once-in-one-hundred-years flood of last year. We don't know where we are in the cycle of floods. We could be just a few years away from a once-in-one-thousand-years flood.

If there is a larger flood than last year, I can just about picture the steel casks clanging together as they float downstream. Maybe something heavy banging into them and making a hole in the steel casks.

I am not anti-electricity. Electricity came to our part of the Fond du Lac Reservation in the 1950s. I can remember just flipping a switch to get light. Gone were the days of kerosene lamps. No more wick trimming or chimney cleaning. I didn't have to fill the lamps with the pungent-smelling kerosene anymore. Just flip a switch and get light.

At first, we listened to the radio, then along came TV. I watched the atom bomb tests on TV. I imagined myself as one of the soldiers climbing out of the trenches, advancing towards the mushroom-shaped cloud. Now my TV lets me know those same soldiers have claims against the government because of the exposure to radioactivity. The atomic veterans believed the government when it said this was safe. Now the government would have us believe that dry cask storage is safe.

What really scares me is the idea of storing radioactive fuel rods in northern Minnesota. I have heard that the geological formations in this area make it ideal for storing killer waste. I have a message for the decision makers—don't even think about it. We are upstream from everyone. A nuclear accident here would poison everybody's water.

Hazel O'Leary, who used to work for NSP, now heads the US Department of Energy. We should be able to figure out her position on the storage questions.

I have a plan for the storage of the killer waste we have now. Store the waste in the backyards of those who were responsible for making it. Make storage a family legacy. When the original responsible person dies, the waste could stay in the family, year after year, until it is safe. The experts say it would only take ten thousand years. Northern States Power executives, state legislators, and federal agency heads could document the safety of dry cask storage by renting out their own backyards.

We don't have to worry about damaging earth, air, and water. The Earth will be here even if we have poisoned ourselves out of existence. The wind doesn't care if it is blowing radioactive dust. The rivers will flow even if they are glowing, even if there is no one to watch them. It's not too far from casks to caskets.

Wednesday, April 27, 1994, 5A
Computer Literacy Important for Indian People

We need to put our electronic moccasin tracks on the information superhighway. There is a revolution going on and, if we don't join, we are going to be left in the dust. I remember the words of Chief Plenty Coups: "With education you are the white man's equal, without it you are the white man's victim."

My dream is to see that every Indian home on the Fond du Lac Reservation has a computer. Not just a computer but access to the information networks. The computers could be linked together for information sharing.

We could advise the decision makers on major issues. Say, for example, the reservation wanted to sell treaty rights to the state of Minnesota. The people affected could let their leaders know how they feel by typing in their answers to a survey. The leaders could explain their reasons for wanting to sell.

Maybe reservation leaders want to get involved in a casino deal with the City of Duluth. Once again the people could be heard on the idea. It would be true democracy rather than the representative democracy we have now. We could vote on every important issue.

One of the advantages gained is we could become computer literate in one generation. If the people had access to the tool, they would use it. We would be better preparing our children for the world they will live in.

We have a long history of adopting new technologies. The gun replaced the bow for taking food. Steel knives last longer than stone ones. Telephones have made the moccasin telegraph operate faster. We play more blackjack than cribbage. We adapt and change to survive in our surroundings.

There are schools that use an interactive computer to teach the language. I think the Anishinaabeg of this rez would use that particular program. One good way to preserve the language is to use it. If people had access to this information, they would use the language more.

The children of the reservation are learning computers in school. They could use those skills to teach their elders how to use the machines. We could have an encyclopedia on a disk in every home. I believe this would add to the quality of the students' homework. The interaction between the generations would add to the strength of the families.

The computer could be used to play video games. That would be a plus when the wind chill is 75 below zero. Our college students could use the computer in their studies. The students could research and write their papers at home. They could show their families what they had learned.

Once on the information superhighway, the people could share information with others around the world. There is a thirst out there for information about the Anishinaabeg.

Maintaining the information system would create jobs. We would need technicians and librarians. Technocrats rather than bureaucrats.

Of course, there are obstacles to every dream. The first is the cost to get on the information superhighway. One way would be to use a small part of the casino profits to pay the initial startup costs. Dedicate a small percentage for the reservation computer network. That would be an easy way to demonstrate to the feds that the gaming profits are being used wisely. Use gaming profits to pour concrete for the information superhighway infrastructure.

The people could use community service to demonstrate their willingness to earn access to the information superhighway. Volunteer hours could be exchanged for computer components, hardware, software, and access. If the people can earn the computer through volunteer labor, they will take care of it. That way it won't seem like welfare or some other give-away program.

The infrastructure is already available for just such a system. Computers are in use in the reservation schools, the casinos, and administrative offices, but we need to bring them to the people. We can't afford to be hitchhikers on the information superhighway.

Wednesday, May 25, 1994, 9A
Casino Gambling Profits Should Go to Purchase Land

In the coming elections on the Fond du Lac Reservation, voters will decide whether gambling profits should be used for a new school.

I say no. We have many worthy causes, and I don't think building a new school is one of them. I have heard that there is state and federal money available sometime in the future. It was just reported in the newspaper that Nett Lake got state money for their school. I suggest we wait for that funding source. We pay federal and state taxes, so it's our money, too.

One of those worthy causes is reclaiming the reservation from the white man. According to the *Cloquet Pine Knot* newspaper, the reservation owns or controls only 22,000 out of the original 100,000 acres. The state and county own 20,000, the University of Minnesota 3,700 acres, and 51,300 acres are owned privately. There's a lot of land on the reservation we can buy back.

Having the voters decide an important question should be news. Traditionally on the reservation, the tribal council decides the weighty issues, then tells the people what they've decided. It wasn't petty, but it is what passed for democracy on the Reservation.

I am not anti-education. I want the best possible education for my children and grandchildren. That is one reason I send my son to a public school off the reservation.

I had one son who attended the Ojibwe school a few years ago. By the end of the school year, all he could say that he learned was if you put a bead on a porcupine quill, it makes a great dart. I thought that was an innovative use of traditional materials, but it wouldn't help him get a job. As a parent I expected more from the school.

I think our reservation school needs to be built from the inside before we start looking at the outside. We need fully qualified teachers and administrators. Anything less would be a disservice to our children. We should use the same standards in use by other school districts.

We need an independent school board. As it stands now the whole operation is run by the RBC. We should make the School Board an elected position. If the School Board is just a rubber stamp for the RBC, nobody wins.

Of course, building a new school would have a positive public relations impact. Our leaders could point to the school anytime a question comes up about gambling. That alone is not a good reason to spend millions.

I've been in the Ojibwe school to make a presentation to the students. The enthusiasm to learn seems to be missing from the school. I don't know what causes it, but I don't think it will be cured by a new building.

I've seen the failure of discipline at the Ojibwe school. It seems like the students are running the school and the staff is just there to watch what happens. Something is backward here.

Putting the gambling profits in the school would not be an equitable distribution of the money. Not all Fond du Lac people have children. There are many reservation students who don't attend the Ojibwe School. Would we be short-changing the people who don't have children of school age? Those who don't send their offspring to the Ojibwe school?

If the referendum passes, I think we should figure out the cost per student then give that amount to each student who goes to another school. That would be an equal distribution of the wealth.

I know the buildings are shoddy and need to be replaced. Maybe we could make some interim repairs until the state or federal money comes through.

Money or a new building alone won't magically improve the quality of education offered by the Ojibwe school. It's got to start from the inside. In the meantime, I'm going to vote on this issue just because I can.

As a Fond du Lac voter, I applaud this new openness in tribal government. Can this be a new trend in the way we do things around here? Is this ushering in a new era for the RBC and the Fond du Lac people? Don't bet on it.

Wednesday, July 27, 1994, 7A
Eagle Feather Worth Taking Stand For

I went trolling for game wardens in Burnette County, Wisconsin. I had an eagle feather hanging from my car's rearview mirror that was clearly visible.

The trolling for game wardens started when they took an eagle feather away from an enrolled Winnebago named John Gauthier-Taborshak. He was followed from his home to his job at the Hole In The Wall Casino where he was stopped by the Wisconsin Department of Natural Resources wardens. Once they had him stopped, they took his eagle feather and wrote him a receipt. They then told him he would be hearing from the feds.

According to warden manager David Zeug, they are holding the feather until the Winnebago man can prove that he is an Indian. Both the feds and the state of Wisconsin say we can possess eagle feathers. But more importantly, our elders say we can.

Game warden Zeug says there is extra sensitivity toward eagles since eighteen of them were found poisoned in northern Wisconsin last April. The poisoned eagles apparently had all their feathers when they were found. Zeug further stated to the newspapers that his department "fully recognizes the rights of Indians to possess eagle feathers. But it's in everyone's best interest that the possession be monitored to protect the eagles and the tribal members access to them."

Just what we need—more "monitoring." The year 1984 was ten years ago and Big Brother is here in the form of state game wardens.

The boat landing protests are behind us, and now we have to prove our identity, so we can practice our religion. Do other people have to prove their identities to practice their religions? Does the priest carry an ID card issued by the pope? Who certifies the Protestants? What about the Buddhists and the thousands of other religions?

If the game wardens are so intent on confiscating eagle feathers, come to a powwow. Stand right where the dancers come in for grand entry. The game wardens would see more feathers than they could count.

It wouldn't be a good idea to confiscate feathers there because of the danger of someone resisting. I know I would resist.

I earned my feather for my service as a grunt in Vietnam. The feather is dressed with the colors of the Vietnam Campaign Ribbon. Yes, I know that I would resist anyone taking my eagle feather.

It doesn't matter if they are armed men with a two-way radio. It doesn't bother me that the game warden can call for back-up. Someone once said if you don't stand for something, you'll fall for anything. Makes sense to me. I will stand for the feather and everything it represents.

There are some things worth fighting for, and for me it is that eagle feather. I see the taking of that feather as a direct attack on our spirituality.

They cannot have my eagle feather.

Now, is there a way to resolve this religious issue short of a physical confrontation? I think so.

First, the game wardens must stop taking eagle feathers from Indian people.

Second, they should return the eagle feather and apologize to the Winnebago man.

Third, spend more time trying to find out who poisoned the eagles instead of harassing Indians.

President Clinton has an eagle feather, so does Senator Daniel Inouye. I saw the senator presented with one during hearings held in Minneapolis last year. Would the game wardens try to confiscate those feathers? I don't think so.

So what is this? A stupid mistake made by armed men acting under color of their badge, or is this the opening round of a new religious war?

In the meantime, I drive a gray Ford Taurus with Minnesota plates. I am unarmed except for that eagle feather and my belief about the importance of eagle feathers to the Indian people. It's part of our religion. You can't buy it or deny it.

Wednesday, August 24, 1994, 7A
Vote on Casino Profits Would Clear Table for Other Issues

People argue about money better than anything.

Here, among the Fond du Lac Band of Lake Superior Chippewa, we have an unusual decision to make.

It is unusual because we have never had to decide anything like this before: What to do with the millions of dollars from gambling?

We're breaking a stereotype here. Indians are supposed to be poor. Isn't that in the Constitution someplace—isn't it written there that Indians gotta be poor?

The profits from the casinos have built up and now we have to decide what to do with the money. Just a few years ago we were trying to decide between USDA commodity pork and chicken for supper. Now we are in the world of high finance, running with the big dogs, as my cousin says.

The Reservation Business Committee has been meeting with the people about gambling profits. I didn't go to the last one held at the old casino building, but I heard it was pretty lively. I heard they called Chairman Sonny Peacock everything but a chipmunk. The question of his ancestry came up. I heard the next meeting is September 15th, 1 PM, at the old casino building.

There are many choices available on what to do with the money. Two months ago we learned in a referendum vote the people didn't want to spend the money on a new school building.

There are Fonjalackers, as we sometimes call ourselves, who have strong opinions about the money.

There are those who want to cut up the profit pie and distribute it equally among all Fond du Lac members. A per capita payment. There are problems with that idea.

First of all, we would be overrun with people claiming to be a three-fifths Fonjalacker on their mother's side—what we used to call the woodwork Indians. They come out of the woodwork when the Indian pie is being cut up. That is one problem. Another one is the tax man. How much would we give to the federal government in the form of taxes? As we know, the feds have got to get their cut.

The ancient cry of economic development is heard. We should use the money to go into other business ventures, some say. Diversify away from gambling because we don't know how long our monopoly will last. Has everyone forgotten the furnace factory or the Fond du Lac Technologies?

Others want to buy land. What a novel idea. We use the

white man's money to buy back our land that was stolen in the first place. I kind of like that one; there is something ironic about it. What a worthy goal—to be able to say we own most of the land on the reservation. At least 51 percent anyway.

Still others want to use the gambling profits to augment the existing programs. The clinics in Cloquet and Duluth can always use the money somewhere.

The Wild Rice Committee could use the money to improve the reservation watershed. That project has been operating on a small scale for the last couple years. A crew of dedicated ricers from Fond du Lac have been clearing ditches of fallen trees, helping water flow. They can always use the money to ensure that we will have the manoomin for the coming generations.

Then there are programs for the elders, programs for the young ones.

So many good ideas for the use of the money.

The best way to settle this weighty question is to let the people decide. Let's vote again. We're pretty good at voting.

Everyone would win and the RBC would get a clear mandate from the people about the gambling profits. They would know where to put their energy.

The people would win because they would be experiencing pure democracy. The voice of the people would be heard.

We should decide quickly, so we can quit talking about money. We should be talking about fighting racism, fighting for clean air and water, protecting treaty rights, and preserving the Anishinaabeg language. Some things are more important than money.

Wednesday, September 26, 1994, 7A
**United States Must Put Own House in Order
before Offering to Aid Haiti**

Why do we hate Haiti? What is so wrong there that we have to risk young American lives?

I watched President Clinton on TV trying to explain the invasion. Neither he nor television news anchors convinced me that it is in our best interest to invade Haiti. What is going on here?

All the high and mighty phrases being used do not justify putting one American life in danger. Words like democracy, justice, and freedom are thrown around like cheap toilet water to cover the smell of this rotten mess.

Several years ago I wrote about the Haitian refugee problem. People were being returned to Haiti because they were economic refugees. At the time I thought it was a good idea. Return the people because they were not political refugees. I also wanted to make the policy retroactive to the year 1600. Send all the economic refugees back to their country of origin. It is now some three years later, and the Haitian problem is still here. The economic sanctions didn't work, so now we will try diplomacy with a bayonet.

I support the troops but not the president.

We are supposed to be outraged because the Haitian police and military are using nightsticks to control the population. From what I have seen on TV, the use of nightsticks was nothing like the Rodney King beating in LA. The US military didn't invade LA to stop the police.

Our troops are armed and have plenty of naval and air support. They are prepared to fight with their small arms and automatic weapons. The question immediately comes to mind: Who the hell is the enemy?

President Clinton says the three military dictators are the source of the problem. He says nothing about the arrogance of the United States. Who gave us the right to decide the future of another country?

The president points to the United Nations resolution as legitimate proof that we belong in Haiti. He is giving us the impression that the entire world is behind our actions. I don't think so.

Any day now the body count of US soldiers will start.

Who will tell the grieving families that their sons and daughters died in the defense of democracy, justice, and freedom in Haiti? Whenever we have a military operation of this size, there are bound to be accidents where people get killed.

Firefights between our troops and members of the Haitian military are inevitable. On the TV news, I saw Haitian militia being trained with M-1 rifles. The weapons were called old as if to mean they could not be used to kill Americans.

In my time in the US military, I carried an M-l rifle. It was accurate to 500 yards and eight rounds could be fired in less than eight seconds. The danger to Americans is there even if only M-l rifles are used.

The mission in Haiti is too vague. Our goals are not defined. It was almost as if we talked ourselves into the invasion, and now we don't know how to stop.

Wait a minute, this is supposed to be a column about Indian issues. This is an Indian issue because we have dual citizenship. We are citizens of our tribal groups and also of the United States. As a citizen of the United States, I am ashamed about the invasion of Haiti.

As a citizen of a tribal group, I am worried because it took so long to build a government-to-government relationship with the United States. Didn't Haiti have such a relationship with the US Government?

All the phrases we hold so dear in our dealings with the United States suddenly have no meaning. If the Haitians can't practice self-determination, what hope is there for us?

I believe the United States should put its own affairs in order before we begin exporting democracy with military force. There are some reservations in Minnesota that do not have democracy. Let us take care of things here first. What happened? Did someone discover oil or uranium in Haiti? I don't hate Haiti or Haitians.

How Good It Would Be to Become the Last Veteran

Veterans Day is coming. It always reminds me of parades.

When I was young, I used to go to parades in downtown Duluth. This was before television, so a parade was big doings. The music from the bands, the soldiers marching, and flags fluttering all added to the excitement. Memorial Day, July Fourth, Labor Day, and Veterans Day were all good reasons to have a parade. For me, one highlight of the parade was waiting for this real old man to come by.

He was identified as the last surviving member of the Grand Army of the Republic. I think his name was Albert Woolson. He had fought for the Union in the Civil War.

When I saw him he wasn't doing much of anything. I don't remember him waving to the crowd; all he was doing was riding and smiling.

I waved at him, though. I knew I was looking at a piece of living American history. This man was alive when Abe Lincoln was president. He had fought in the Civil War that I read about in my school history books.

As an adult, I wondered about him and his long life. Did he read a newspaper that reported the hanging of the thirty-eight Dakota in Mankato? Where was he when General Custer met Crazy Horse and Sitting Bull? Was he in Minnesota when the Anishinaabeg drove off the Fort Snelling troops at Sugar Point? Was he shocked when the Lakota were slaughtered by the US Army at Wounded Knee? Did he have children or grandchildren in the Spanish American War? What did he really think of World War I and II?

That old man was a veteran of war and life.

I became a veteran after the Vietnam War. I served with the 3rd Battalion, 9th Marines. After our thirteen-month tour, we came home. We didn't get a parade. Instead, we got blamed for losing an unpopular war. We were the visible symbol of the failure of America's foreign policy. The veterans who returned their medals to the US government were on the evening news. Vietnam veterans reported that they had been spit on by American citizens after the war.

Life was too difficult for some who came home after the war. Veterans killed themselves at an ugly rate. Lt. Lewis B. Puller, Jr., the son of Marine legend Chesty Puller, reported that more Vietnam vets have committed suicide than actually died in war. That particular tragedy also struck my family. We buried a brother. He died from what is now called posttraumatic stress disorder.

I believe those Vietnam veterans who are still alive should be looked up to as examples of the strength of the human spirit. We endured and survived the whole Vietnam fiasco.

Once again, my peers are dying. This time it isn't enemy gunfire that is killing them. Suicide is not taking so many of them anymore. What is killing them now is the painful legacy of Agent Orange.

I just came back from a funeral at Fort Snelling. A relative was buried there. He left a wife and children much too early. The color guard fired their rifles then Taps was played. The notes of the mournful music bounced off the rows of white tombstones. I saluted like the other veterans in the crowd of mourners. A grateful nation gave the family an American flag. When that was over, the Dakota people said goodbye to one of their warriors. This veteran had made a claim against the government because of his exposure to Agent Orange. The claim was denied, and his appeal was pending until he died of lymphoma.

It is a good idea to honor the veterans, but a better idea is to quit making veterans. More than half of our military is around the world placing themselves in danger. Why do we keep making veterans? Who is responsible for this? I think the president and Congress make the decisions that create more veterans. The citizens are at fault because we placidly allow our young ones to be sent to dangerous places. This is true even though we have to stretch to justify using American force.

That old man who was a veteran of the Civil War is gone. I've decided that I want his job. I want to ride in a parade as the last surviving veteran of the Vietnam War.

Wednesday, November 23, 1994, 7A
How You Can Celebrate Thanksgiving
Every Day of the Year

Pssst, hey buddy, do you know where we can score a couple of Pilgrims?

I heard that old story about Indians showing the Pilgrims how to survive here. They had a meal together, as the story goes.

Thanksgiving is coming, and once again we're looking for Pilgrims to help us celebrate our feast. In years past, we always started looking too late and found ourselves without Pilgrims for the holiday. We couldn't hold our heads up among family because we were Pilgrim-less on turkey day.

Maybe it's because I am confused by the string of holidays. As we enter the harvest season, they seem to go by faster. Labor Day, then that one in October we don't celebrate, and then Halloween. I always get Halloween's black-clad witches confused with the black-wearing Pilgrims. I think I got it straight now. The witches are the ones with the pointy hats, and the Pilgrims have shorter ones. Are there any other differences between the two? Who gets the black cat?

Some historians say that Thanksgiving started with Governor Bradford of Plymouth Colony in 1621. I believe that is only one version of the stories about Thanksgiving.

We know from the stories that the first people of this continent were having thanksgiving feasts long before the newcomers waded ashore. As if this continent's history started when the Pilgrims got here after the boat ride. My cousin calls Pilgrims the first boat people. He wants people to remember who owned the rock the Pilgrims stepped on when they landed.

Nevertheless, we will remain true to the story, and that is why we must invite Pilgrims to feast with us. Over the years it is getting harder and harder to find Pilgrims. The only place we hear them mentioned anymore is in a John Wayne movie, as in, "Put the wagons in a circle, Pilgrim."

Alas, Americans have forgotten the original reason for the holiday. Today it means football games and shopping for that next one called Christmas. I wonder if the Redskins or Chiefs are scheduled to play on the fourth Thursday in November?

I'm starting to see advertising for Christmas buying already. The countdown to shopping days has begun. Can the Christmas lighting contests be very far behind? I'm always amazed by that annual event. How do they determine the winner? Do they go by the amount of electricity consumed or artistic merit?

Of course, Thanksgiving means the elections are over, and we won't have to listen to that stuff for a while.

Thanksgiving is always a good time to reflect on what we should be thankful for. For our family, it is our health. My family is fortunate in that we continue to enjoy good health, mental and physical. We feel pretty good about having a long history on this continent, also.

Sure, we'll have the traditional turkey at our feast, but it will be augmented by wild rice and moose meat. As we are eating, we will remember that 1854 treaty rights were used to bring part of the feast to the table. I hope we can find some Pilgrims to feed.

As we eat the wild rice we will be reminded of the many generations of Anishinaabeg who used wild rice in thanksgiving feasts before 1620.

We will eat and then continue to try to understand the newcomers to this continent.

Why so grim, Pilgrim? Is it because it is difficult to be thankful about pollution?

I am thankful the nuclear wastes at Prairie Island haven't started leaking yet. Oh, sure, there was that little bitty leak of radioactivity last month, but that was nothing. It was so small Northern States Power didn't even notify the Dakota people nearby. I am thankful that I live upstream from their steel cask storage experiment. I am thankful for the good water I drink.

For me, Thanksgiving Day is celebrated every day. I am reminded daily of the gifts from the one who made us all—Pilgrim or Anishinaabeg.

Wednesday, December 28, 1994, 7A
Renewed Interest in Ojibwe 40 Years Late but Welcomed

As a young man, I was sent to the Federal Boarding School at Pipestone, Minn., where the use of the Ojibwe language was discouraged. We had Ojibwe pounded out of us and English pounded in. The policy at the time was: educate the heathens and destroy the language.

The original language of the Anishinaabeg was spoken at home and at ceremonies, but not at the school.

Our parents and grandparents knew what was happening at school, so they went out of their way to speak English to us. They were trying to keep us out of trouble and were preparing us for the future. We learned English because it was the only language used at school.

Language speakers made fun of us because we couldn't speak Ojibwe. They would ask us what kind of Indians we were if we didn't speak our language. I couldn't answer them because I was too busy learning English.

Along the way I felt a sense of loss because I could no longer understand when my elders were talking. I especially hated it when I knew they were talking about me.

It seemed like the generation before me was ashamed of the Ojibwe language. They would never speak it when white people were around. For the most part, no effort was made to teach young ones the language. Ojibwe went underground and stayed there a long time.

Poet Adrian Louis said something like: "Respect our elders? They're the ones who got us in this mess." At times, I felt that way about the Ojibwe language speakers.

Most of us learned a few words and phrases because we were around Ojibwe speakers. We learned Ojibwe, but not enough. Mostly we learned imperatives like: don't, be quiet, sit down, don't cry, eat, or go to bed. It is hard to carry on a conversation using just commands.

One guy said for the first eight years of his life, he thought his name was Gego, the Ojibwe word for don't.

There is a renewed interest in the Ojibwe language. Instead of getting beat for using it, we can now get college credits. Most colleges in the Midwest have classes that teach the Ojibwe language. Head Start and elementary schools on the reservations encourage the use of our language.

This is a good idea, but I'm bitter I had to wait forty years to see it happen.

Wilf Cyr from the Fond du Lac Community College has a glossary in his computer. I think anyone can access the program and learn from it. There are many language tapes available. I see them advertised in the native newspapers. I use a tape when I drive to the Twin Cities. I get a two-hour language course every time. My vocabulary is getting larger; I have more tools to use to express myself.

We encourage the use of the language in our home. We try to use all the Ojibwe words we know in everyday conversation. We answer the phone in Ojibwe. It has been interesting since we started doing that. My mother-in-law, a fluent Dakota speaker, uses Ojibwe when talking to her daughter on the phone.

Todd Orjala from the University of Minnesota Press recently sent me one of their newest publications: *A Concise Dictionary of Minnesota Ojibwe*. It contains more than 7,000 of the most frequently used Ojibwe words. The words were selected from a database of 25,000 words. It was put together by Earl Nyholm and John Nichols.

From the dictionary I learn Ojibwe words for: television, mazinatesijigan; Duluth, Onigamiinsing; newspaper, babaamaajimo-mazina'igan; Minneapolis, Gakaabikaang; and United States, Gichi-mookomaan-aki.

I like to say I speak and understand the Ojibwe language, but my vocabulary is very limited. With resources like the new University of Minnesota Press dictionary and Ojibwe speakers in the community, I can continue to learn. I will spend the rest of my life learning Ojibwemowin. My children and grandchildren will learn also.

INDIAN ISSUES: 1995

Wednesday, January 25, 1995, 7A

When We Reform Welfare, Save the Bureaucrats

Welfare this and reform that.

Everyone says we must reform the welfare system. Taxpayers, politicians, and the Sunday morning TV talking heads all say we must reform.

Welfare recipients are being indirectly blamed for the multibillion-dollar federal deficit. The people getting welfare don't like the system because it robs them of their self-esteem. The current welfare system breeds dependency. What incentive is there for people when the first comes once a month, every month, year after year?

Getting welfare money is easy. Simply grovel, fill out the forms, and wait for the check. Bare your soul, financial and otherwise, and you could qualify for the free money.

Of course, if you have a car given to you when Aunt Martha died, you'll have to sell it. Recipients must prove they are truly needy. Got to get rid of the toys like snowmobiles, boats, land, insurance policies, family heirlooms, and anything else of value before you qualify. The free money doesn't pay for the dignity taken away.

Taxpayers don't like paying for the increased cost of the welfare system. Is there a law someplace that says taxes must always go up?

Politicians are now using words like "welfare reform" to mollify middle-class taxpayers. In the last couple of years, they were talking about crime, but now it is reform that is being promised.

I may have heard it wrong, but someone told me that Republicans have taken out a contract on America. I also heard that Barney and Big Bird are worried.

Don't even bring up the defense budget because, now

that the Cold War is over, we have to spend more money on different kinds of wars. Defense contractors are still slopping at the public trough.

But wait, there is a side of this welfare reform issue we haven't looked at yet. I read recently that the welfare dollar is spent roughly like this: one-third for the recipients, and two-thirds for the administration of the programs.

Now, two-thirds of every welfare dollar buys a lot of bureaucrats. No one has spoken out for them. If we are not careful, bureaucrats could become an endangered species. The downsizing of welfare agencies would dramatically affect the ranks of loyal civil servants. Some might even lose their jobs.

We must do everything possible to ensure that those loyal civil servants do not go without a paycheck. I wonder what the economic impact would be if suddenly the middle-class taxpayers at the agencies were thrown out of work. Would they have to sign up for welfare?

In the interest of efficiency, we must take steps now to protect the paychecks of the bureaucrats. Some of the civil servants have been working at the agencies for years. That means their job-seeking skills are rusty. We must begin immediate outplacement services for the civil servants.

The caseworkers, financial workers, section heads, and directors must be rewarded for their years of loyal service. We've got to set up job hotlines and job fairs for the bureaucrats. We need workshops on resume writing and interviewing skills.

We must do everything possible to take care of the civil servants. We don't want them to go postal on us. Who needs more disgruntled workers?

Maybe the college recruiters could visit the agencies. I'm sure higher education would help take the sting out of being unemployed. Civil servants could become students if they correctly fill out the forms for the grants and loans.

The military could use bureaucrats. A horizontal transfer to the military would preserve the paychecks of some loyal civil servants. I'm sure the Marines would change their slogan to "We're looking for a few good bureaucrats."

In our rush to reform the welfare system, we must not forget those who get the bulk of the welfare dollar. No effort is too great when lifestyles are at stake.

Wednesday, March 22, 1995, 5A
Similarities, Differences Found in Scotland Are Surprising

We were not exactly innocents, but we went abroad anyway. My wife, Pat, and I were invited to Scotland to talk to people who wanted to learn about Indian reservation life in America.

We flew from Minneapolis to London. The temperature was 41 below on the other side of the DC-10 cabin wall. We were traveling at 550 miles per hour, and I didn't want to know the wind chill.

In London, we landed at Gatwick Airport. We took a little train to a big train at Kings Cross Station. That is when we learned that we were called Red Indians from America. The train took us up through the middle of English history to Scotland. We saw the countryside. There was green moss on all the trees. The trees themselves looked kind of scrawny compared to northern Minnesota. I thought Robin Hood would have had trouble hiding from the sheriff in these woods.

Eventually we got to Aberdeen after an eight-hour train ride. The North Sea was at the bottom of the street, and we noticed they have a different kind of cold. Damp, unlike the dry below zero cold in Minnesota. We froze until we got acclimated. The apartment (flat) didn't have a TV (telly). What freedom—no OJ for two whole weeks.

The people in Scotland didn't have any trouble understanding us. I think American movies and TV helped. We were a half sentence behind in understanding them the whole time we were there. We asked people to speak slowly.

The next morning we crawled out of bed to crawl around

a castle. The stonework was amazing at Dunnottar Castle. It had a dungeon where 140 people were imprisoned during one of the wars. It was a nice place to visit, but I wouldn't want to live in a dungeon there.

One night we were out eating with some friends. I had to use the bathroom (loo, WC) so I asked a civilian for directions. When I got there I noticed the international symbols for men and women were on the doors. One wore pants and the other wore a skirt. I was in Scotland, land of the kilt, so I couldn't decide which was which. Finally, in desperation I chose one, which turned out to be the correct choice. That is when I noticed the toilet flushing handle was on the other side. I did an informal check and it was universal. All the toilet handles are on the opposite side. I tried to tell my wife about this, but she didn't care.

In Scotland, they have really old history. We visited some stone circles that were erected thousands of years ago. The stone circles were built so they could be seen from another circle on the next hill. It is unknown who built them or what they were used for.

The Scottish people have a history that is similar to our own. The highlanders were thrown off their land, it was against the law to speak their language, and they were treated as something less than human. Thousands of them came to Canada and America during the clearances.

We went to Loch Ness to see the monster. He was cleverly wearing a fishing boat disguise. We got pictures of the Loch Ness monster with his fishing boat hat. What realism, I thought. It looked exactly like a fishing boat. He didn't fool us; we know a monster when we see one.

There are fake medicine men peddling Indian ceremonies in Scotland. One man called himself Pretty Painted Arrow. He was in Aberdeen a couple of weeks before us. The newspaper reported that he left town with another man's wife. We know a rent-a-shaman when we see one.

Scotland was clean, the people were friendly, and we

thoroughly enjoyed ourselves. We gave talks at a five-hundred-year-old university. My wife spoke to a women's group. Museums, churches, and libraries all invited us to talk. I think we got the better part of the deal. We learned more about the Scottish people than they learned about us. We are looking forward to our next trip because we were invited back.

Aye, I'll have another wee dram of that single malt.

Wednesday, May 24, 1995, 7A
Former Vikings Coach Rotten Treaty Expert

Bud "No Super Bowl" Grant is now a treaty expert. I just read his guest column published on the opinion page of the Saint Paul Pioneer Press. As an Anishinaabe, I must respond.

I don't know how a football expert becomes a treaty expert. Do you suppose they talked about treaties in the huddles? I don't think so. Coach Grant must have learned about treaties since he retired from the game.

I just can't take him seriously since I saw a picture of Grant in a book called *Homeless Dreams*. He was pictured wearing beadwork and paint on his face. He had what looked like ermine tails hanging down from the beadwork. In the text he says, "As a boy growing up, I would have liked to have lived with the Indians and experienced their way of life. It always bothered me that in the movies they were always the bad guys and always lost the fights they were in. I wanted to help them win."

As they used to say in the old Perry Mason movies, "Exactly when was it when you were lying?" Coach Grant, are you saying the book is a lie when you wanted the Indians to win? Your statements about treaty rights make me think you don't really want the Indians to win.

Fine, let's get rid of the treaties. We'll go back to the way things were before they signed the damned things. That means Grant would have to leave. So would the Vikings and everyone else who is not Anishinaabe or Dakota. But before they leave, I would insist they return it to the way they found it. Clean up the mess that is now called Minnesota. Start with the plants that make electricity and radioactivity.

Grant talks about Mille Lacs Lake. He calls it "the premier fishing lake in Minnesota." I've seen the bottom of that lake. I went spearing in Mille Lacs with other members of ALF, the Anishinaabe Liberation Front. I saw parts of fish houses, a screen door, a padlock, and a lot of beer cans on the bottom of Mille Lacs. Make sure that gets cleaned up before you leave, Coach Grant. It used to be a lake when we owned it. Now it is a liquid landfill.

In his writing on treaty issues, Grant frequently mentions money. According to his view of the future, if the Indians win, property values would go down, sales tax revenue would also dive. He states, "Some real estate agents predict a mass exodus of cabin owners and other recreational property owners from the area."

He might be a bit of an alarmist there. If the Mille Lacs people win in court, they won't rape the resources. Remember, Coach, we have lived here for centuries. The exploitive way of looking at the resources is not our way. We didn't invent strip mines, pavement, or shopping malls. We invented biodegradable canoes.

I don't think Coach Grant understands the concept of dual citizenship. We are citizens of the United States and our tribal groups, too. His writing makes me think he doesn't see us as Minnesota citizens. Coach Grant says the state of Minnesota is being generous because it helped direct millions of dollars to tribal government in federal and state assistance. Grant mentions Minnesota officials who signed lucrative gaming monopoly compacts. He says for these reasons Mille Lacs people shouldn't be suing the State of Minnesota.

The state has been trampling on treaty rights for years. That doesn't make it right. I am glad Mille Lacs is fighting for treaty rights in the courts. I am even gladder that the

Anishinaabe from what is now called Wisconsin are in the lawsuit. For too many years we allowed the imaginary lines to keep us separate. Treaty rights do transcend state lines. The treaty rights were in use before there was something called Minnesota.

Coach Grant, I am honored to be your opponent in this treaty rights struggle. I am doing it for future generations of Anishinaabe. In the meantime, do you think you could come up with a game plan for cleaning up Mille Lacs at least? I'll help—I have a canoe and a spear.

Wednesday, July 26, 1995, 7A
New York Museum-Goers Eager to Learn about Anishinaabe

Contrary to some published reports, we did not go to New York for vacation. We went there to work.

My wife, Pat, and I were invited to the National Museum George Gustav Heye Center in New York City.

We were there to demonstrate how we make birch bark fanning baskets. Anishinaabe people have been making these baskets for centuries. We learned how to do it from the elders. Each year we teach at least five others what we have learned about basket making. The baskets are used to winnow wild rice and are made from three gifts from the Creator.

The first is birch bark. It is getting harder to find good bark. We share the birch trees with firewood cutters and loggers. An insect called the bronze borer has been blamed for the dead trees seen everywhere in northern Minnesota. They look like white skeletons among the surrounding green trees. I have to walk farther than I used to. The bark is easy to peel for about six weeks of the year. If we remove the outer layer carefully, the tree continues to grow.

We use green willow for the frames of the baskets. It grows everywhere, so it is easy to find.

The baskets are sewed together using basswood bark. The trees grow in clumps, so it is also easy to find what we need. We gather the material all at the same time. Going to the woods is like going to the mall. We pick up everything we need on one trip.

We demonstrated basket making at the new museum that opened last October. Before we started, we toured the museum. There was a collection of Anishinaabe beaded bags that were selected by Earl Nyholm. The beauty of the bags made me proud to be Anishinaabe.

There were a lot of people coming through the Museum. They seemed eager to learn about basket making as done by the Anishinaabe. We answered many questions about birch bark baskets. Sometimes the questions would go beyond baskets and into gambling, treaty rights, environmental racism, or life on the reservation.

At least once a day we would be recognized as American Indians. People would stop us on the streets to ask questions about us and our lives. One cab driver took a $10 bill out of his wallet for us to autograph. I signed as Kevin Costner, and I believe my wife used the name Pocahontas when she signed.

Of course, we met another Anishinaabe while walking the streets of New York. He was from Winnipeg, and I asked why he left. His cryptic answer was "Warrants." We were able to share a meal with him. Indians always seem to find each other in crowds.

We rode the Staten Island Ferry both ways. On the way to the island, we saw the Statue of Liberty. I wondered why she had her back turned to the original people of this continent. We also saw Ellis Island where so many immigrants came through. It looked like a prison or boarding school. The lights were just coming on in the city on our ferry ride back.

The subways were interesting. We rode underground for fifty city blocks and when we came up, we were still downtown. There were people flowing on the streets, streams, rivers, lava flows of people. We didn't recognize anyone we knew.

Naturally, we went to Times Square and Wall Street. We took pictures of tourists taking pictures. We didn't get mugged.

I'd like to think that we educated some people about the Anishinaabe from northern Minnesota. The museum staff members we worked with were satisfied with our effort.

The National Museum of the American Indian bought one of our baskets and took still pictures and videos of us working. Now we can brag that one of our baskets is in the Smithsonian. The staff members are already talking about our next visit.

Yes, we'll go back to New York. We'll go back when my great-great-great-grandson graduates from college.

Wednesday, August 23, 1995, 9A
**Marine Reunion Leaves Vietnam Veteran
Reflecting on War**

America loves veterans. We must because we keep making so many of them.

Why does America love to go to war so much? If we can't find someone to fight, we fight ourselves. Witness the Civil War when in some cases brother fought brother. I could never understand how a war can be civil.

Sure, the original inhabitants had war before the white man came, but it was nothing compared with the way we have been fighting wars since this nation was formed.

The rest of America's history is filled with war and war stories. It would be too difficult to list all of the bloody confrontations between the native people and the United States. In our tribal history, we know that the Anishinaabe won the Battle of Sugar Point that was between us and the troops of Fort Snelling.

Look at how many ways we celebrate wars and veterans. Our calendar has two major holidays a year because of war. First is Memorial Day, when we honor the dead veterans from America's wars. The next is Veterans Day, where we remember the living veterans. In between we have Flag Day in June and the 4th of July.

For the last couple of years, we have been celebrating World War II. A year ago, we commemorated D-Day and the invasion of Normandy. Now we are in the middle of VE and VJ Day celebrations.

Clifton Rabideaux, Sr., Frank Thompson, Pat Smith, Emmet Thompson, Harvey Danielson, Gene Thompson, Joyce Loons Troseth, Amos Pellerin, John Sharlow, and Blaze Savage traveled to Washington, DC, to take part in the dedication of the Korean War Memorial. These Fond du Lac Band members fought in that forgotten war. There were others from the reservation who died before the dedication.

A Vietnam veteran, I took part in a thirty-year reunion. Grunts (infantrymen) from India Company, 3rd Battalion, 9th Marines got together.

The doings were at a plush hotel in Arlington, Va. The perimeter was set up in a hospitality suite where there was a sign-up sheet. Each grunt who signed in was careful to read the whole list looking for someone he knew.

In the suite, we looked at pictures, slides, helmets, the company guidon, maps, NVA flags, flak jackets, and jungle boots. All these reminded us of our time in the war. Mostly, we looked at each other's eyes.

We went everywhere together. During the war, the India Company rode on tanks, amtracs, and in choppers. This time we rode in an air-conditioned bus. One stop was the Iwo Jima memorial. When I looked at the statue, I thought of Ira Hayes, a Pima Indian who took part in the flag-raising. I know that American Indians serve in the military at a greater rate than any other population group.

We went to the Wall. Names, so many names, of our friends.

Another stop was at Marine Barracks, Washington, DC. As any Marine can tell you, the address 8th and I is at the top of the chain command. It is where the commander sleeps and the Silent Drill Platoon performs. The Marine Corps band plays music there.

We left the barracks with the sound of taps still in our ears and hearts.

There was a banquet back at the hotel. We had speeches, music, and dancing. Mostly, though, it was Marines telling war stories. We knew we would get together again sometime.

It was a good reunion, but there were bad parts also. I wondered about the missing faces. I worried about some of the men who were there. They are still troubled about what they saw and did in the war.

After the reunion, I felt sad, like I had left my best friends behind.

Maybe if we didn't talk about it so much, we wouldn't have so many wars. It is a part of our vocabulary. We have had War on Poverty, War Drugs. I'd like to see a War on War. Nobody hates war as much as a veteran.

Wednesday, September 27, 1995, 7A
Taxing Casinos Latest of White Man's Stealing from Indians

Tax the Indian casinos?

A pox on your House and Senate for even thinking of it.

American Indians have given and given to help make this country what it is today. The land stretching from the Atlantic to the Pacific was once ours. The natural resources that made America a world power were stolen from us, and I won't forget that.

Does anyone besides me remember that we were supposed to get a dime a ton for the iron ore that was taken from northern Minnesota? That promise was remembered in the oral tradition but mysteriously disappeared when the words were written down in the treaties.

Now I read that the federal legislators are rushing a bill through that would allow them to tax our casinos. The profits would be taxed at the rate of 34 percent. Hearings were not held, and those most affected were not heard. It reminds me again of Mitch Walking Elk who sings, " . . . and when they want what we got, they just change the laws,"

Lately I've heard us called semi-sovereign. My American Heritage Dictionary defines sovereignty as: 1. supremacy of authority or rule, 2. royal rank authority or power, 3. complete independence and self-government. I cannot find a definition for semi-sovereign. I always thought sovereignty was an absolute, like perfect or pregnant. Do we say someone is semi-pregnant?

We are being asked to clean up after someone else's budget mess. Taxing the casinos to help balance the budget after the saving and loan debacle, the bloated military budgets, and the Medicare hemorrhages is a bad idea.

A recent *St Paul Pioneer Press* and KARE-TV poll of a random sample of 805 voting adults found that 57 percent want Indian casinos to share their profits with the state. I would like to commission a poll among American Indians and ask them the same question. What do you suppose that poll would show?

Simply because a majority wants it doesn't make it right. This is manifest destiny all over again. Didn't we already sing this song?

America is so used to thinking of us in stereotypes that it can't stop. Only a small percentage of the casinos make enough money to give their members a per capita payment. Most casinos invest their money in schools, sewage systems, roads, and economic development. The stereotype exists that we are all getting rich at the expense of the white man.

While I appreciate the irony of Indians making money off white people, I don't think it should be shared. They didn't share when they were raping this continent, so why should we?

The state of Minnesota was not there to put up the money for the casinos. Neither was the federal government. They're acting like parasites. They risked nothing, but they want to share the profits. What in the wide world of sports do they think they're doing? Do you suppose they forgot we are now educated, and it is not as easy to fool us?

Instead of taxing casinos, I think we should tax foreign aid. Take a small percentage of the millions of dollars that we send to other countries. Or better yet, let's tax the military budget.

While we're at it, let's tax the state lotteries. After all, they're in the same business as we are. If the states are not taxed on their gambling revenue, why should we be the ones to pay?

I already pay a lot of taxes as an Indian on the reservation. I am liable for income taxes, both state and federal. Whenever I buy a gallon of gasoline, I pay 20 cents in state taxes plus 18 cents in federal taxes. I pay sales taxes that go directly to the state. I even pay part of Minnesota Power's tax bill. It is itemized on my light bill every month. Taxing casinos to balance the budget is wrong. There are more honorable ways to raise money than to single us out for special taxes.

Wednesday, October 25, 1995, 7A
Ojibwe Writer Proud of Stand against Racism in Baseball

The World Series is here and I'm not going. I like baseball, but the screwball idea of using Indians as mascots is an error. In my field of dreams, it wouldn't happen.

I balk at the thought of seeing the tomahawk chop on television again. I strike out when trying to explain what it means to my grandchildren. I walk when I see the fans wearing turkey feathers and paint. I am forced out of the room when I see the people waving foam tomahawks.

Those who think we are being honored by using Indian mascots must have a franchise on stupidity. They must have sacrificed their common sense and will never enter my hall of fame. Personally, I think they should be wrapped in wet horsehide and put in a batting cage.

My family and I were at the World Series when the Braves were playing the Twins. We were pitching an educational message to the fans, but I see they didn't catch our message. Nevertheless, I will continue to fight against racism even if we go into extra innings. I hope we will continue to advance on this important issue. I want to get rid of the spikes of racism. America needs a change in its attitude toward the original people of this continent.

There are hundreds of tribes of indigenous people here in America. In spite of our differences, we must form a league to combat this evil. We must shut out racism every time we see or experience it. We are not rookies; in fact, we are veterans at it because we have hundreds of years of experience.

I bet Pete Rose would like the idea of respecting each other more than we do now. I think Joe Jackson would have given up his shoes if it would have helped. Even Jackie Robinson would break into the major leagues of happiness if we struck out racism in baseball. I would give Kirby Puckett a pennant to wave if we got rid of dumb nicknames. If Ted Turner had a single idea to change the double faced attitudes about us, it would triple my respect for him. We could run home and tell our children. Joe DiMaggio had a smile on his face after fifty-six consecutive hits; my smile would be even bigger if we didn't have to hear the hey-ya song any more. I don't want to even talk about Chief Noc-a-homa and Chief Wahoo.

One reason given for not changing the names is the cost of such a move. In these days of multimillion dollar players and stadiums, that doesn't make sense. Who says it is good business to demean us? How many times do we have to tell the owners of the teams we don't like what they do? When the Braves were in Minneapolis the last time for the World Series, I had an idea. I thought we should use some of our gambling gold to take out ads during the games to promote mutual respect. I hope our leaders use that idea. I wouldn't even care if they said it was their idea. I know that an ad campaign takes a while to put together, but if we are serious about fighting racism, we should spend the money. This problem won't go away by itself. If we don't do it, who will?

Some people say this is a small issue and we should spend our time and energy on more important things. I disagree. We must pop up and strike out against racism regardless of what form it takes. Offensive nicknames do not contribute to our self-esteem. We need things that make us feel good about being one of the original people of this place now called America.

For the duration of the World Series, I will only read the *Minneapolis Star Tribune* because it is one of the two newspapers in the country that do not use politically incorrect nicknames. I guess I will also have to give up radio and television until this craziness is over. I will continue to eat Baby Ruth candy bars, however.

The World Series is the end of the baseball season for this year, but football is on deck. Next we have to wind up against the Redskins.

I am proud to show my children and grandchildren I took a stance against offensive nicknames. I want them to know that racism is not the great American pastime.

Wednesday, November 22, 1995, 7A
So Many People Wanting to Be Indian
Tied to Connectedness

Why do so many people want to be Indian? As I travel, I meet people anxious to tell me about their Indian connection.

I was in Madison, Wisconsin, last week at a bookstore. I was there to listen to a friend read poetry from her new book. After the reading, while my friend was talking to her fans, I stepped outside for a smoke.

A woman I never saw before came up and asked me if I was an Indian. When I told her I was Anishinaabe, she started telling me about her connection to Indian people.

She said she was part-Cherokee on her mother's side. It was a dark family secret, but she was anxious to find her roots. I murmured sympathetic noises during her sad tale of child abuse, neglect, and denial. The conversation was barely minutes old and already I was hearing terrible secrets. I didn't know what to say to ease this woman's pain.

The conversation left me troubled. Why did she think I could help her find answers to her questions?

Then I remembered that this had happened quite a few times before.

I was in Minneapolis. A man walked up and asked if I was an Indian. I told him I was Anishinaabe. He started talking about how the Indians respect the land like his brother did. The man then went into a long convoluted story about his brother, the hunter. When he died, they cremated him, loaded him in shotgun shells, and scattered him over the land. It was a fitting memorial for a man who loved the land like the Indians.

The man was beginning to get misty-eyed as he told me the story. I don't know why I was selected to hear the dead brother story. I listened, then shook his hand. As I was walking away, I remember wanting to ask if they hit anything with their brother.

My friends and family tell me that the same thing happens to them when they travel. We trade stories back and forth about the stories we hear from people who are anxious to prove their Indian connection.

There are quite a few people claiming a Cherokee connection. That has been going on for years, but lately I am hearing people claiming to be Chippewa, Dakota, and even Lakota.

So why is this happening? It can't be the gambling gold because we have been hearing this long before the gambling started. Maybe people sense our feeling of being connected to a family.

We are rooted here. Our families have been here a long time, and we prefer to live together. In my small village, I am related to more than half of the people. I bask in the security of living among relatives.

For example, I ran into my brother at the store. I said if it gets colder, we'll have to break out the long johns. He said he has had his on for a month now.

A small connection, but a reminder that we are all in this together.

Living among family isn't always a happy utopia. We have the usual collection of oddballs, misfits, and those who are not flying in formation. We also have a sister who just graduated from the University of Minnesota—Duluth. We have a brother, once a grandson here, now a grandpa.

The feeling of family can't be bought with money. Anishinaabe people always have lived close to family.

Perhaps it is the feeling of family, of belonging to something.

I was waiting in an airport for a connecting flight. While I was sitting reading a newspaper, I felt like someone was looking at me. It was a small boy about five years old. He had black hair and brown skin and eyes. His mother came up and took him by the hand and told him not to stare.

She asked if I was Indian. I told her I was Anishinaabe. She said her son was an Indian, maybe Lakota, maybe something else. She told me in great detail about the adoption process they went through to get this child. The woman said she took the boy to a lot of powwows so he could be proud of his culture and heritage.

I wanted to tell her there was a lot more to it than that, but my plane was loading. I smiled at the kid like he was my grandson. He smiled back.

TRANSLATED POEMS

Ishkonigani-odaabaan
(Rez Car)

Translated into Ojibwe by Melvin Geyshick and Rick Gresczyk
Gaa-aanikanootamowaad Ojibwemong: Melvin Geyshick miinawaa Rick Gresczyk

Ashi-niizhwaaso-biboonagizi
Gichi-aabadizi nawaj igo dash niibowa
Ombiigwewe nawaj igo dash wiin bemisemagak
Niizhwaaswaak-niimidana ashi niizhwaaswi
Nenoojinaagozi, anooj izhinaagozi,
Gaawiin idash detibisejig osayensiwag, bebakaaniziwag,
Niin dash niizhwaazo- maagizhaa ishwaaso- debenimag
Ingikendaan niin sa ishkwaaj ge-ishkwe-dibenimag
Aaniin ezhiwebizid?
Aaniish naa
Mii dash awasonaaago
Gii-pangisin aadikwe'igan
Gaawiin anokiimagasinoon bizindamoo-makak
Idash anokiimagad awazowin
Odaabaani-apabiwinan ogii-waabandaanan niibowa
    ojiidan
Dash wiin ojiidi-mashkikiwinini gaa-waabandang
Ingwekiwebinaan aabaabika'igan ezhi-maajiibizod
Ninagaawebishkige ezhi-noogibizod
Aaniin gaye ge-izhichiged odaabaan?

Nindooshtigwaani-mashkikiwininiban (Shrinking Away, or My Dead Shrink)

Translated into Ojibwe by Melvin Geyshick and Rick Gresczyk
Gaa-aanikanootamowaad Ojibwemong: Melvin Geyshick miinawaa Rick Gresczyk

Ingii-waabanish gii-miigaazoyaan imaa gii-miigaading
Dash zanagad ji-bimaadiziyaan ishkwaa-miigaading
Gaawiin ingashkitoosiin ji-nibaayaan niizho-diba'igan
Ingii-kotaaj ji-ayaanziwaan nimbaashkizigan
Zegaabandamowinan dibikak miinawaa giizhigak
Nindanaamindizowin, niniisaanendamowin
Ingii-aapiji-giiwashkwebiishk apane
Ashi-zhaangaswaak-ingodwaasimidana-ashi-
    ingodwaaswi
Miinawaa gii-ikidowag ogimaag imaa
    zhiimaganishi-ozhibii'igewigamigong:
Gaawiin gii-miigaadiwinagasinoon imaa VietNam-ing.
Gaaiin ingii-wiidookaagosiig
Dash ingii-miinigoog
    ozaawi-giigidoo-biiwaabikoonsi-mazina'igan
Ingii-odaapinaa bezhig oshtigwaani-mashkikiwinini
Naanimidana daswaabik ingodiba'igan ingii-anoonaa
Ingodwaak niizhtana-ashi-naanwaabik ingii-
    shooniyaake endaso-giizis
Ingodwaaching ingii-waabandimin ji-gikenindiyaang
Ingii-noondawaa ge wiin omiigaadiwini-bimaadiziwin
    miinawaa onoojininiwewin, gii-miigaadiwaad
    omaamaayan miinawaa dash wegodogwen
    waa-tibaajidang
Biinish igo geyaabi indaa-gii-anokiikaanig ashi-
    zhaangaswaak-zhaangasimidana-ashi-zhaangaswi
    indaa-gii-anokiikaanig
Ingii-pakibinaa ji-anookikaanig, ingii-ishkwaataa'aa
Gaawiin ingii-te-diba'osii
Gaawiin ingii-mino-doodaagosiin

Ingodwaaso-anama'e-giizhik idash nindooshtigwaani-
     mashkikiwinini gii-nisidizo
Howa!
Gaawiin eta go indanaamindizowin gii-miigaazoyaan
     imaa gii-miigaading
Mii dash noongom wenji-oshki-anaamindizoyaan
nindooshtigwaani-mashkikiwininiban gii-nisidizod
Mii dash apegish nawaj mino-anokiiwin ayaamaan
Indaagii-waabamaa miinawaa
Mii dash gaa-inendamaan indani-minochigemin
Ganabaj ingodwaaching geyaabi wayaabandiyaang
     indaa-gii-wiidookawaa
Mii wapii gikendamawiziyaan ji-bimaadiziyaan
     ishkwaa-miigaading
Niin booj ji-anokiikaadamaan

Manoomin
(Rice)

Translated into Ojibwe by Megan Noodin
Gaa-aanikanootamowaad Ojibwemong: Megan Noodink

Semaa zaaga'iganing
megwa bagidinigeyaang.

"Aambe" kidod bizaanabo
manoominag wewebikweniwag.

Ind'manoominikemi miinwaa, miigwetchwigo Manido.

Manoominan zinigonanan giizhik.

Atitemagad manoomin
gii wiikoongetonid biboong.

Wazawashkan ezhinaagwadan gaag.

Ondaanimad zaaga'iganing
migizi, niizh kaakazheaandwag bineshensag
miziweshkaa giizis zhoomingwed.

Nindawenamigog maamwi dagoshinowag
dibaajimonid gaa ezhiwebag zaaga'iganag.

Biintoonanid biisamanoominan megwa
baapiyaang, dibaajimoyaang, mikwendamaang.

Wenpanad ji-debendaamaang
gete-Anishinaabeg dodemag
manoominikegoba oma.

In'gii gichinendamomi maajtaayaang.

Oshme in'gii gichinendamomi giizhitaayaang
miijim oondoondanid jiimaaning
miinwaa Anishinaabe-zaagidiwin jiimsowensan.

SHINNOB JEP

CAST:

AL TREEBARK

The host of the game show from the Fond du Lac Reservation. He wears a hat, ribbon shirt, black jeans, and moccasins.

FRANKLIN LAKE

A contestant on the show and an American Indian Movement warrior. He keeps his long hair in a ponytail and wears a black t-shirt, blue jeans, and sneakers.

TRADISH IKWE

A contestant on the show who lives with the seasons on the Fond du Lac Reservation. She wears her long hair in a single braid with a beaded hair tie, turquoise necklace, beaded earrings, and white tennis shoes.

JOHN JOHNSON, JR.

A contestant on the show who was adopted out. He has his hair cut short and wears the typical white man's uniform—black pants, black shoes, white shirt, and necktie.

SETTING:

The stage contains a bingo table. It is covered with a Pendleton blanket used as a table cloth. On the table are three table top podiums. Each podium has a microphone.

The host has a stand-alone podium. It can be decorated with Ojibwe beadwork stencils or a colorful blanket. It has a microphone.

There is a stand-alone chalkboard that is used to list the game categories and dollar amounts.

Behind everything is a large red banner. Painted in the center are the words "SHINNOB JEP."

SHINNOB JEP

As the audience enters, they see a dimly lit set and hear singers and a drum (optional). It is a powwow song, a 49er. As the lights come up, the singers and drum fade.

The announcer walks in from behind the audience's seats, greeting the crowd, waving to people he knows. When he gets to the stage, he turns to the crowd.

AL TREEBARK

Biindigen, come in. Welcome to Shinnob Jep, the show that tests your knowledge on being a Shinnob. We didn't make our casino connection yet so we're still a low budget show. Here's your host, Alllllll Treeeeeebark.

The announcer now becomes Al, as he walks around the podium he takes off one hat and puts on another different colored one.

Al Boozhoo, boozhoo. Nimino-ayaa gaye niminwendam omaa

ayaayaan noongom. Nimino-ayaa gaye niminwendam omaa

ayaayan noongom. Nimino-ayaa gaye niminwendam omaa ayaayeg noongom.

Are there any of my relatives here? Ever wonder how the contestants for Shinnob Jep are picked? Nepotism, pure nepotism. What good is nepotism if you can't nepit. I picked these people to take part in this show. Always looking for contestants for this show.

Well, let's play Shinnob Jep. Our first contestant comes to us from the mean streets of Minneapolis. He is enrolled at the White Earth Reservation. Franklin spends his time at the Peacemaker Center making war on racism. Help me welcome Franklin Lake to Shinnob Jep.

Treebark leads the applause.

Franklin comes out and walks to his podium, waving at the crowd, and gives Al a tall clenched fist salute, Al gives him a half-assed one in return.

FRANKLIN
Boozhoo, brother. I knew I could make it up here. I was just telling the White Earth Reservation Tribal Council I was going to be on the show. They might want you to bring the show to the Shooting Star Casino. I'll let you know.

AL
Mii gwech. Our next contestant is from the Fond du Lac Reservation, where she makes maple syrup in the spring, dances at powwows all summer, goes ricing every fall, does beadwork all winter, and watches kids the rest of the time. Welcome Tradish Ikwe to Shinnob Jep.

The host leads the applause.

Tradish comes walking out and goes to her podium, waving at friends and relatives on both sides of the crowd, then nods at Al.

TRADISH
Boozhoo, Al. Good to see you again. How is your maw and dad?

AL

They're both good.

to the audience

Our parents went to boarding school together.

to Tradish

Last time I saw you was at that powwow in Bena, wasn't it?

TRADISH

cupping a giggle

Yah, you were there with that blond woman with the big, I mean, really big . . . cameras.

AL

mumbling to his feet

I remember, I was helping her with a research project.

TRADISH

Oh, is that what they call it nowadays?

AL

Daga bizaan, let's move on. Our last contestant comes to us from Edina, Minnesota. He is an engineer at Control Data and just learned he was adopted by a white couple when he was a little guy. He is enrolling at Leech Lake and finding his real family. Welcome John Johnson, Jr., to Shinnob Jep.

Tradish and Franklin switch name plates. so John isn't standing between them because he looks like a Chimoo-komaan. John sees them, Al doesn't.

JOHN
Hello, Al, I mean, Boozhoo. I hope I do well on your show.

AL
We hope so, too. We all know how the game is played. Unlike TV's JEOPARDY!, which does it backward, here we ask the questions—you give the answers. There is one Daily Double in this round. Here are the categories: Ricing, Powwows, Tribal Councils, Higher Education, Casinos and Gambling, and Race Relations. John, you lost the coin toss—you have to go first. Pick a category.

JOHN
I'd like Higher Education for one dollar, Al.

AL
Here's the question. What is the first fiction writing course taken by students?

JOHN
The financial aid forms.

AL
That's right, for a dollar. Your choice again.

JOHN
Higher Education for two dollars, Al.

AL
Okay, why go to summer school?

FRANKLIN
Financial aid all year 'round.

AL
Correct for two bucks. Pick a category, Franklin.

FRANKLIN
I'd like Race Relations for five dollars, Al.

AL
For five dollars in Race Relations, who invented deodorant because they needed to?

JOHN
The BIA?

AL
Wrong, you're in the hole for four bucks. Franklin, who invented deodorant?

FRANKLIN
The white man.

AL
That's right for five, pick again.

FRANKLIN
Tribal Councils for three.

AL
The question for three dollars in Tribal Councils is, when do the dead come to life?

TRADISH
Just before the election.

AL
Right, the dead come to life long enough to vote. That's three dollars for Tradish. Your turn to choose.

TRADISH
I'd like Ricing for four hundred, oops, I mean four dollars, Al.

AL

Here's the question, what does milky rice mean?

TRADISH

It means you are ricing too early. Jeez, I thought everyone knew that.

AL

Right again, every year some clown sets the opening of the ricing season too early. Pick a category.

TRADISH

Race Relations for three dollars.

AL

For three dollars, respond to the following statement: my grandmother was a Cherokee Princess.

TRADISH

Yah, right.

AL

That's wrong. Anyone else?

JOHN

Oh . . . that's . . . nice.

AL

Correct for three dollars, you now have four. Pick again.

JOHN

I'd like Race Relations for four, please.

AL

In Race Relations for four, respond to the following statement: my grandmother was a REAL Cherokee Princess.

JOHN
Oh . . . that's nice.

AL
Incorrect, you're back to zero. Anyone else want to respond to "my grandmother was a REAL Cherokee Princess"?

FRANKLIN
Who gives a fuck?

AL
Who gives a fuck is the right response to "my grandmother was a real Cherokee Princess." Your turn.

FRANKLIN
Bekaa, bekaa. Am I supposed to use that F-word on your program?

AL
Sure, we'll just pretend this is cable or satellite TV. Still your turn.

FRANKLIN
Powwows for five, Al.

AL
Okay, for five, what is the difference between a contest and a traditional powwow?

FRANKLIN
About a thousand bucks for first place.

AL
Wrong, although we'll check. Nope, the judges say it might be true at some powwows but not all of them. Anyone else want to try? What's the difference between a contest and

traditional powwow?

TRADISH
One is for the money, one is for the people.

AL
Right for five bucks, pick again.

TRADISH
I'll try Ricing for five, Al.

AL
In the category for Ricing, what can you use if you don't have a cast iron parching kettle?

TRADISH
Your uncle's kettle or a galvanized tub?

AL
Correct. Your turn to pick again, Tradish.

TRADISH
Give me Casinos and Gambling for two dollars.

AL
I was betting we'd never get to this category. Okay, for two dollars, what is a good gambling tip?

JOHN
Gas up the car before you get to the casino.

AL
Right, give that man a roll of nickels. Pick again, John.

JOHN
Casinos and Gambling for three dollars.

AL

For three dollars, what is the player's responsibility at the casino?

FRANKLIN

To get as much money as possible.

AL

Hai', wrong, although it is a nice wish. Anyone else?

TRADISH

To move the money from one slot machine to another.

AL

That's right for three dollars.

TRADISH

Let's have Race Relations for two.

AL

The question is, why don't the Chimooks understand the Shinnobs?

TRADISH

They haven't been here long enough.

AL

Sad but true. What has it been? Five hundred years ago? Your turn, Tradish.

TRADISH

Casinos and Gambling for four, daga.

AL

Okay, for two rolls of nickels, what are the odds you'll meet someone you owe money to at the casino?

FRANKLIN
Even money. I know, it happens to me all the time.

AL
Correct for four dollars. Your turn again right after these commercial messages. We got to pay the bills, so we can keep playing Shinnob Jep. Want to help, Tradish? C'mon, it's easy, just hold this placard.

Tradish holds up placards

Hey gamblers, having trouble getting to the casino? Maybe your car was repossessed in a dispute over the payment plan. Maybe your lawyer says to wait before you try driving again?

Whatever the problem, War Pony Tours is the solution. We make the circuit of Minnesota casinos quicker than anyone. One hour stops at the following casinos: Black Bear, Firefly Creek, Fond du Luth, Fortune Bay, Grand and Grand again, Grand Portage, Jackpot Junction, Lake of the Woods, Little Six, Mystic Lake, Red Lake, River Road, Shooting Star, Treasure Island, and White Oak.

We have other cars strategically placed, so you can continue the trip when the first car dies. Wake up any driver from War Pony Tours for the death ride of your life.

Tradish changes placards

Have your kids been taken away by the county, again? Have you set the state record for DWI arrests, again?

Holdem, Robbem, and Leavem can help. We've been helping Shinnobs since we found out they can pay their legal bills. Get one of our "Get Out of Jail Free" cards. Call 1-800-SHY-STER for an appointment. Holdem, Robbem, and Leavem is an equal opportunity exploiter of the legal system since 2007.

Holdem, Robbem, and Leavem is here to help.

Tradish puts down placards

And now back to the game.

FRANKLIN
I'll try Tribal Councils for four dollars.

AL
For four dollars, why don't incumbents get 100 percent of the vote?

FRANKLIN
It costs too much to buy that many votes.

AL
Correct, it just costs too much to buy that many votes. Pick again.

FRANKLIN
I'd like a Higher Education for three dollars.

AL
Okay, in that category, how long does it take to get a four-year degree?

JOHN
Four years?

AL
Wrong, anyone else know how long it takes to get a four-year degree?

TRADISH
Six to twelve years.

AL
Absolutely right. Another?

TRADISH
I'll try Casinos and Gambling for three dollars.

AL
Casinos and Gambling for three is a Double Daily. You can risk up to twenty bucks. This is the only Double Daily in this half of the game.

TRADISH
Shoot the works, I'll try twenty.

AL
For twenty bucks, what's the difference between praying in church and praying at the casino?

TRADISH
At the casino you really mean it.

AL
Right again, pick a category.

TRADISII
Give me Higher Education for four dollars, Al.

AL
Okay, for four dollars, what is better than a computer for studying?

JOHN
A really smart roommate.

AL

Right. I used to have one. Your turn.

JOHN

Tribal Councils for five dollars, Al.

AL

For five, how many relatives of the Tribal Council does it take to cut the grass or shovel snow?

TRADISH

Two or three.

AL

Gaawiin, anyone else want to try? How many relatives of the Tribal Council does it take to cut the grass or shovel snow?

JOHN

All of them.

AL

Eya', it takes all of the relatives of the Tribal Council to cut the grass or shovel the snow. Next category, please.

JOHN

I'd like Tribal Councils for two bucks.

AL

What is Plan B to ensure the outcome of the election?

JOHN

Election Boards appointed by the Tribal Councils.

AL

That's right for two bucks. Give that man another roll of nickels. Another category?

JOHN
I want Casinos and Gambling for five, Al.

AL
How do you start a fight at a casino?

JOHN
Sit next to a non-smoker.

AL
Correct, just sit next to a non-smoker. Your turn.

JOHN
Higher Education for five, Al.

AL
What's better, a grant or a loan for college?

JOHN
A grant, at least that is what worked for me.

AL
Right you are. Pick again, daga.

JOHN
Race Relations for a dollar.

AL
The last question in Race Relations is: do you mind if I ask
what ah tribe, ah band, ah group you belong to?

TRADISH
No.

AL
Incorrect, a good answer but not the one we're looking for.

Anyone? Do you mind if I ask what ah tribe, ah band, ah group you belong to?

JOHN
Yes, I do mind.

AL
Correct for one dollar. Pick again.

JOHN
I'd like Powwows for four dollars, daga.

AL
In that category name four things that contribute to a good powwow?

JOHN
Good dancers, good drums, a lot of giveaways, and honor songs.

AL
Close, but not the answer we were looking for. Anyone else?

FRANKLIN
Good water, good food stands, a quiet place to camp, and freshly pumped powwow toilets.

AL
Keereckt for four. Pick again.

FRANKLIN
Give me Tribal Councils for one dollar, Al.

AL
You can't buy a Tribal Council for one dollar. It takes much more than that. In all seriousness, for one dollar in that category, who gave us Tribal Councils?

JOHN

The federal government, the Feds.

AL

Right. The 1934 Indian Reorganization Act. Your turn to choose.

JOHN

Casinos and Gambling for one dollar.

AL

For one dollar, should you hate someone who wins on a machine you just left?

JOHN

No, it's never right to hate someone, especially a stranger.

AL

Gaawiin, haven't played the slot machines much, have you? That'll cost you a dollar. Anyone else? Should you hate someone who wins on a slot machine you just left?

FRANKLIN

Eya', for a little while anyway.

AL

Correctamundo. Give that man a half roll of nickels.

Okay, before we get started on Shinnob Double Jep, let's recap the scores and chat with the contestants. Tradish is leading with thirty-six dollars, Franklin is second with six- teen dollars. John is sucking hind tit with twelve bucks.

Franklin, on your card it says you're enrolled at White Earth. Tell us an election story.

FRANKLIN

An election story, eh? Well, one time my cousin and I were guarding the cemetery, but the dead got by us and voted the same dictator into office, again. I like voting, last election I voted sixteen times. My cousin was greedier and voted twenty-three times. At a hundred bucks a vote, we both made money on that election. I like getting Ben Franklins for Franklin on Election Day.

AL

Thank you for sharing that with us, but shouldn't you be telling that story to the Inspector General of the Interior Department?

FRANKLIN

I already did. They interviewed me several times, and I may get subpoenaed to Federal Court.

AL

Thanks, we'll be looking for you in the newspapers.

John, your card says that you just found out you were once a Shinnob but were raised white. Did that make it difficult for you?

JOHN

Sometimes. Now I understand why I wanted to choke my sister's rabbit; it wasn't violence: it was hereditary. I never got sunburnt like the rest of the family either. In the photo album I stick out like a blueberry in a glass of milk. I'm taking day courses in Indian Studies and night classes in the language. I want to connect with my real family.

AL

That's great, John. Glad to have you back with us.

Tradish, on your card under marital status it says you are unremarried. Does that mean we can try again?

TRADISH

Nah, you had your chance. Where is your blonde with the big . . . cameras?

AL

It ended before the project did. We don't see each other anymore. But enough about her, what are you doing this weekend?

TRADISH

I'll be washing my hare, my snowshoe hare. Seriously, what did you have in mind for the weekend? I might be around.

AL

Well, Wild Rice Breath, they have bingo at the Black Bear Casino, want to join me there? They gave me some packages for mentioning their name on the show. You still like bingo, don't ya?

TRADISH

I like bingo a little bit, especially at the Black Bear. I can join you there Friday night, Saturday afternoon and evening, Sunday afternoon and evening, or Monday afternoon and evening.

FRANKLIN

Hey, this is Shinnob Jep, not the Dating Game. Aaniin dina?

AL

Gaawiin gegoo. Now that we got that squared away, let's go back to the game here. The categories in this round are: US History, Trick or Treaties, Trick or Treatment, Body Language, Sugar Bush, and Rez Cars. Franklin, you gave me the last correct answer, so it's your turn again. Pick one.

FRANKLIN

I'll try US History for one dollar, Al.

AL

For one dollar, who defeated General George Armstrong Custer at the Battle of the Little Big Horn?

FRANKLIN

That's an easy one, Crazy Horse, a Lakota.

AL

That's right, pick again.

FRANKLIN

Give me Rez Cars for a dollar.

AL

Here we go, who never drove a Rez Car?

FRANKLIN

Crazy Horse, a Lakota.

AL

Correct, your turn again.

FRANKLIN

I'd like Trick or Treatment for a buck.

AL

For one dollar, who never went to treatment?

FRANKLIN

Crazy Horse, a Lakota.

AL

Boy, you really know these subjects, don't ya? Go ahead, pick another one.

FRANKLIN
I want Trick or Treaties for a dollar.

AL
Name a famous Indian who fought during treaty signing times?

FRANKLIN
This is too easy. Crazy Horse, a Lakota.

AL
Once again that is the answer we were looking for. It's still your turn, Franklin.

FRANKLIN
Give me Rez Cars for two dollars.

AL
For two bucks, what is the payment plan for a Rez car?

FRANKLIN
Everything down and nothing a month for the life of the car.

AL
Are you gonna let anyone else play? But speaking of payment plans, I have to take another commercial break here.

Tradish comes over to help without being asked. John goes for a smoke. Franklin is just looking around. Tradish holds up the Niiwin placard while Al reads from a card.

Got a big giveaway coming up? Talk to Niiwin from Niiwin's Tipi Poles. He makes balsam and tamarack poles for tipis. They are handmade up to forty foot in length and are smooth as a baby's ass.

Niiwin likes bartering, so he'll trade poles for damn near anything. Money, wild rice, money, dance regalia, money, maple syrup, money, bingo packages, or money. He has rentals and loaners.

Tipi poles do make an ideal gift for those relatives that get per capita and have everything. When you need something to hold that canvas up, try Niiwin's Tipi Poles. Remember, our poles are biodegradable and will not harm the environment. No sweat, Global Warming.

John returns to his podium. Franklin is still looking around talking to the audience members. Al holds up the Boogid placard, while Tradish reads the next commercial message.

TRADISH
Have your kids been playing sword fighter with your knockers, again? Has your old pole seen one too many seasons?

Al moves the placard to cover his groin.

Boogid's Wild Rice Tools is the answer. We're always ready for ricing because we make professional grade tools at mud-bottom prices. At Boogid's we use straight grain cedar for the knockers and carve them to fit you. Our spruce-diamond willow poles can be used to push a Lake Superior ore boat. At Boogid's we make ricing tools your grandchildren will fight over. As my grampa used to say, ricing is never more than eleven months away.

AL
And now back to the game. Franklin, it's still your turn.

FRANKLIN
I'm on a roll here. Rez Cars for three, daga.

AL
Will a Chevy wheel fit on a Ford car?

FRANKLIN
No, it will not.

AL
Hay', wrong answer. Anyone? Will a Chevy wheel fit on a Ford car?

TRADISH
I suppose it will if your . . . hammer is big enough.

AL
Eya' Tradish, pick your category.

TRADISH
Rez Cars for four dollars, Al.

AL
In that category, what do you use to replace a broken radio antenna?

TRADISII
A wire coat hanger.

AL
Good answer, your turn again.

TRADISH
US History for two, daga.

AL
For two dollars, who invented the BIA?

FRANKLIN
Someone who was really mad at us.

AL
Right, your turn to choose.

FRANKLIN
We haven't done Body Language yet. I'll try that one for two bucks.

AL
Demonstrate someone giving directions. How would you say, "That way, around the corner, to the right."

TRADISH
Like this.

Her lips and chin point straight, then lips turn to the right.

AL
That's right. You could get a job as a tour guide or at a kissing booth. Your turn.

TRADISH
I'll try Trick or Treatment for two dollars, Al.

AL
Here's the question. Why go to treatment?

FRANKLIN
Job security for my cousin Wiinag, the counselor.

AL
We'll accept that. Choose again.

FRANKLIN
Trick or Treaties for three, Al.

AL
Okay, how can we improve the treaty making process?

JOHN
We write them in our language then tell the President what it says after he signs it.

FRANKLIN
Ho waa, good answer niij.

AL
That's right. I wish we could have done that with all of them. Pick again, John.

JOHN
Trick or Treatment for three.

AL
In that category, what is the 13th AA step?

JOHN
To quit bragging about the previous twelve steps.

AL
Correct. Your turn to choose.

JOHN
I'd like US History for three dollars.

AL
Okay, for three bucks in US History, who did you cheer for during the Civil War?

FRANKLIN
Both sides!

Franklin raises both arms, followed shortly by Al, Trad-
ish, and John, who do the same.

AL
Right again. Your category, please.

FRANKLIN
US History for four bucks.

AL
Who invented canoes?

FRANKLIN
We did, Ho waa, nitaawichige.

AL
That's a good answer, pick another one.

FRANKLIN
Trick or Treaties for two frog skins

AL
How long does the grass grow and the river flow?

FRANKLIN
Until the white man needs the land and water.

AL
Eya', that's right. Your turn to choose.

FRANKLIN
That was a good one. Trick or Treaties for four, please.

AL

That's one of the two Double Dailies. You have thirty-two dollars. You can wager the entire amount, if you like.

FRANKLIN

Do it all, we didn't come in here half-stepping.

AL

Okay, the question this time is in Commods Spanish. Provide the English translation for: degermed harina de maiz.

FRANKLIN

The answer is "enriched yellow corn meal."

AL

Eya', that's correct. You now have sixty-four dollars. Pick again.

FRANKLIN

We haven't done Sugar Bush yet. Give me that one for a dollar, daga.

AL

For one dollar, how did you know he was new at the sugar bush?

JOHN

He was tapping a basswood tree.

AL

Eya', your pick.

JOHN

Sugar Bush for two.

AL
In that category, how did you know he was new at the sugar bush?

JOHN
He kept looking for a bush made of sugar.

AL
Eya', pick again.

JOHN
Sugar Bush for three, please.

AL
For three bucks, how did you know he was new at the sugar bush?

JOHN
He kept saying, "Why do you do this? You can buy syrup at the store."

AL
Eya', we like that answer. Try again.

JOHN
I like this category. Four dollars in Sugar Bush

AL
The question this time is: How did you know he was new at the sugar bush?

JOHN
He burnt himself while playing with the fire.

AL
Eya', how do you know these things? I thought you were

from Edina and worked at Control Data?

JOHN
I am from Edina, but I went to the sugar bush for the first time this year, and I made all of those mistakes. Can I have the last question in that category?

AL
Okay, for five bucks. How did you know he was new at the sugar bush?

JOHN
He went home before noon.

AL
Eya', that's right. You cleaned up in that category. Pick another.

JOHN
I'll try Body Language for three, please.

AL
For three bucks, how did you know she was mad at him?

FRANKLIN
She was staring daggers and making fists at him with her hands in her pockets.

AL
That's right, Franklin. I thought you went to sleep over there. Glad to see you back in the game. Okay, your turn to choose a category.

FRANKLIN
Trick or Treatment for four, Al.

AL

The question is, quote the source, "He was taking my inventory?"

TRADISH

That's from the AA's fourth step, Al.

AL

Eya', absolutely right. Way to go. Your turn, Tradish.

TRADISH

I'd like Trick or Treaties for five, Al.

AL

That is the other Double Daily. You have forty-nine dollars. You can risk the entire amount.

TRADISH

Nah, since I was eighteen when we first went out, I'll bet eighteen dollars.

AL

Now that is a good reason. The question is in Commods Spanish. Provide the English translation for "jarabe de maiz."

TRADISH

Easy beans, that's "corn syrup."

AL

Right again. You're really smart. You're now tied with Franklin at sixty-four dollars. Pick again, we have a few questions left.

FRANKLIN

Still trying to snag, Al?

AL

Bangii etago. Pick me. I mean pick a category, Tradish.

TRADISH
US History for five, you old rat hide.

AL
Hey, I didn't think you cared enough to call me a rat hide.
Apii ji go mii gwech. Oh yah, we're still in the game here. For
five bucks in US History, say one swear word.

JOHN
pounding the podium

Manifest Destiny

AL
Correct, your turn, John.

JOHN
I'd like Rez Cars for five, Al.

AL
Here we go, tell me a Rez Car story.

JOHN
I'm at a little bit of a handicap here because I drive a new
Volvo, the 340 DL model. The one with windshield wipers
on the headlights. I heard a story last week. Let me see if I
got this right.

I knocked a hole in one of my pistons, and every time I
cranked it, the dipstick would come shooting out of the
engine.

John shows us how the stick flew

It was fun . . . until the dipstick hit a Highway Patrolman's
squad car.

AL

Wow, not bad, told just like the driver of a Rez Car. We'll give you five dollars for that story. Pick again.

JOHN

Body Language for five.

AL

Demonstrate one way Shinnobs greet each other in a crowd.

JOHN

I saw two Shinnobs doing this yesterday at the Mall Of America.

makes eye contact with Al, tilts his head back and forth a half inch

AL

Close enough. I'd nod back at you. That answer is good for five bucks. It's still your turn.

JOHN

Trick or Treaties, Al.

AL

All right. Who owns the rights guaranteed in the treaties?

JOHN

Not the Tribal Councils, but the generations of Anishinaabeg to come. The ones not born yet.

AL

Great answer. I want to give you four dollars of my own money for that answer.

TRADISH

I'll chip in three bucks myself.

FRANKLIN
Me, too. Here are my three dollars.

AL
All right, that leaves both of you with sixty-four bucks. John, you now have sixty-one dollars. We're running out of time here. Pick a question.

JOHN
I'd like Body Language for three, please.

AL
Demonstrate the stroke used to knock wild rice.

JOHN
I saw this in one of the movies at the university.

As he reaches out for the rice with his left arm and knocker, he leans it over the canoe and strokes it with his right hand, which then reaches out for the rice that is stroked twice. He continues until stopped by Al.

AL
Bekaa, bekaa. Are you sure you haven't done this before? It looked like you were on your way to half a sack, at least. That brings your total to sixty-four dollars.

That's the end of this round leaving the Shinnob Final Jep question in this category—ricing. Write down your wagers and answer to this question:

What is yet another Shinnob ricing snagging line?

Tradish and Franklin write down their numbers and answer to the question. John looks perplexed until Tradish and Franklin show him their answers. John then writes down the answer.

AL
Time's up . . . John, show us your answer.

JOHN
I wagered it all and wrote down. . . . Wanna go ricing? You bring your knockers; I'll bring my pole.

AL
That gives you one-hundred and twenty-eight dollars. Franklin, show us how much you bet and your answer.

FRANKLIN
I did the same thing as he did. I bet it all. Here is my answer: Wanna go ricing? You bring your knockers; I'l bring my pole.

AL
You're tied with John at one hundred twenty-eight dollars. Tradish, don't tell me you did the same thing too?

TRADISH
Sure, that was an easy one because I hear it all the time. I bet sixty-four dollars too.

shows her answer

Wanna go ricing? You bring your knockers; I'll bring my pole.

AL
It looks like we have a tie game here. Nobody loses; you're all winners. Thanks for playing the game.

to the audience

Thank you all for coming to Shinnob Jep. Mii gwech.

to Tradish

Tradish, can I have your phone number?

TRADISH
Sure, bekaa.

She takes a small piece of birch bark out of her pocket, folds it, and begins biting it with her eye teeth. She looks at it, folds it again, and bites once more. She continues. When she is done, she hands the bark bitten number to Al.

FRANKLIN
Hey John, we're starting a new drum group at the Peacemaker Center. Want to join us, learn how to sing, maybe hit a few powwows this summer?

JOHN
That'd be great. Here is a card with all of my numbers, home, office, cellphone, beeper, fax, webpage, and email. Will we see you there, Tradish?

TRADISH
Maybe. Why don't you stop by the house next fall? We can teach you how to make rice, you know, finish it the old time way.

gives Al the nod

AL
I've never seen a three way tie before. Wonder why it happened?

JOHN
Maybe when we share information and wisdom, we all win. Mii sa iw.

ABOUT THE AUTHOR

© Ivy Vainio

Jim Northrup is an award-winning journalist, humorist, poet, and playwright. His syndicated column, Fond du Lac Follies, was named Best Column at the 1999 Native American Journalists Association convention, and he holds an honorary doctorate of letters from Fond du Lac Tribal and Community College. As a Vietnam War veteran, Jim integrates his experiences into his writing and speaks to both veteran and Indian communities across the country.

Jim lives in Carlton, Minnesota, on the Fond du Lac Indian Reservation.